AF215169

First published in Great Britain in 2026 by Hamlyn, an imprint of Octopus Publishing Group Ltd, Carmelite House, 50 Victoria Embankment London EC4Y 0DZ www.octopusbooks.co.uk

An Hachette UK Company www.hachette.co.uk

The authorized representative in the EEA is Hachette Ireland, 8 Castlecourt Centre, Dublin 15, D15 XTP3, Ireland (email: info@hbgi.ie)

Copyright © Octopus Publishing Group Ltd 2026

Distributed in the US by Hachette Book Group, 1290 Avenue of the Americas, 4th and 5th Floors, New York, NY 10104

Distributed in Canada by Canadian Manda Group, 664 Annette St., Toronto, Ontario, Canada M6S 2C8

All rights reserved. No part of this work may be reproduced or utilized in any form or by any means, electronic or mechanical, including photocopying, recording or by any information storage and retrieval system, without the prior written permission of the publisher.

ISBN 978-0-60064-014-1
eISBN 978-0-60064-018-9

A CIP catalogue record for this book is available from the British Library.

Printed and bound in Great Britian.

10 9 8 7 6 5 4 3 2 1

Publisher: Lucy Pessell
Senior Designer: Alicia House
Senior Project Editor: Katie Button
Assistant Editor: Samina Rahman
Production Controller: Sarah Parry

This FSC® label means that materials used for the product have been responsibly sourced.

RECIPES FOR
Pickling &
Preserving

A Collection of Timeless
and Trusted Recipes

hamlyn

Contents

Introduction

Homemade pickles and preserves can elevate simple meals and turn seasonal produce into delicious treats that can be enjoyed any time of the year.

Pickling and preserving is a rewarding and time-honoured tradition that taps into our burgeoning interest in living and eating more mindfully and sustainably. Setting some time aside to chop, shred and simmer is a way to slow down and settle into the rhythms of the seasons.

If you have a glut of tomatoes from your garden, or you want to transform some foraged goodies into gorgeous gifts, or simply want to preserve some of the delicious vegetables you bought at a market, this collection of over 80 recipes offers all sorts of inspiration.

If you are new to preserving and want to ease in gently, a chutney is perhaps the best place to start as there are no tests for setting required. Preparing jams and jellies requires a little more attention, but the finished results are well worth the care. The Basics section overleaf offers some helpful pointers.

The Basics

Types of preserves

CHUTNEYS – are sweet and sour and made with vinegar, sugar, spices and fresh and/or dried fruits, and usually with a base of chopped onions plus tomatoes or cooking apples. All the ingredients are added to the preserving pan at once, then cooked 'low and slow' until thick. Serve with cheese, cold meats or sausages, or add to sandwiches.

PICKLES – these can be made with vegetables, first soaked in a dry salt mix or brine to draw out the juices, then rinsed and packed while raw, or blanched for a few minutes with flavoured vinegar or a thickened spiced vinegar. Some fruits can also be pickled in a sweetened vinegar mix. Serve with salads, cold meats, cheese or smoked fish.

JELLIES – a crystal-clear preserve, best made with fruits that have pips or seeds, or are fiddly to prepare, as the fruit needs just chopping with no need to peel or core first. Cook gently just covered with water until soft, then strain through a jelly bag. Add 500 g (1 lb) sugar for every 600 ml (1 pint) of strained liquid. Boil until setting point is reached. Delicious served with roast meats, game, grilled fish or cold ham.

JAMS – typically made just using fruit and sugar, unlike a jelly these are not strained and have chunks of fruit.

FRUIT CHEESES – made with a fruit purée and 375–500 g (12 oz–1 lb) sugar to every 500 g (1 lb) of purée. The mixture is cooked gently until reduced and very thick. This sets firmly and is best spooned into oiled wide-necked jars. Serve sliced as part of a cheese course.

RELISHES – these can be cooked or uncooked, and tend to be hotter and more intense than a chutney. Serve with curries or cold meats. Uncooked relishes must be stored in the refrigerator and served within a day or two of making.

Equipment

PRESERVING PAN – most have sloping sides with, ideally, a spout to help you pour. They can vary in size but are generally around 30 cm (12 inches) across the top and about 18 cm (7 inches) deep.

JELLY BAG – this cone-shaped bag can be made from linen or fine nylon mesh. It has strings or long loops at the top so that the bag can be suspended. It is great for making jellies.

OTHER ITEMS – useful kitchen equipment includes scales, a roasting tin, wooden spoons, a ladle, lemon squeezer, fine sieve, vegetable peeler, chopping board and knives.

Testing for set

Generally you will be able to tell if set is almost there as the preserve will begin to lose height as it boils in the pan, and large bubbles will begin to form on the surface. It is important to watch the pan closely, but it usually takes 10–20 minutes to come to setting point.

When you think it is ready, remove the pan from the heat and test by dropping 2 teaspoons of the hot preserve onto a plate that has been chilled in the freezer, allow to cool for a minute or two, then run your index finger through it. If the top wrinkles and a path remains briefly, it is ready.

Jarring

What better way to recycle than to reuse your empty jars? Soak them and their lids in a bowl of warm soapy water to remove any odours, especially if reusing jars that have contained vinegar, then scrub the jars well inside and out, taking care to clean inside the top of the lids. For preserves made with larger fruits, such as pickled peaches or plums, you may prefer to pack the fruit into larger wide-necked springclip jars. These are available in a range of sizes and must be used with the rubber ring to ensure a good seal.

Sterilize all jars and screw-top lids after washing and just before filling. Rinse well with hot water to remove any soapy residues, drain and then stand them in a roasting tin. Warm in a preheated oven set to 160°C (325°F), Gas Mark 3, for 10 minutes.

Alternatively, wash your jars in a dishwasher and use while still warm, but make sure they are perfectly dry before filling.

Storage

Most preserves can be stored for 6 months or longer if kept in a cool, dark place. Choose a cupboard in the kitchen away from heat or light.

Chutneys taste even better if left for 2–3 weeks before use so that the flavours mellow.

The Classics

Autumn Harvest Chutney

MAKES 6 jars
PREPARATION TIME 30 minutes
COOKING TIME 1½ hours

1 kg (2 lb) mixed green and red tomatoes, roughly chopped
500 g (1 lb) red plums, stoned and roughly chopped
1 marrow (about 750 g / 1½ lb), peeled, halved, deseeded and diced
500 g (1 lb) onions, roughly chopped
100 g (3½ oz) sultanas
300 ml (½ pint) distilled malt vinegar
250 g (8 oz) granulated sugar
1 tablespoon tomato purée
2 teaspoons hot paprika
2 teaspoons English mustard powder
1 teaspoon salt
2 teaspoons peppercorns, roughly crushed

Add all the ingredients to a preserving pan, stir to combine, then cook, uncovered, over a gentle heat for 1½ hours, stirring from time to time, but more frequently towards the end of cooking as the chutney thickens.

Ladle into warm, dry jars, filling to the very top and pressing down well. Disperse any air pockets with a skewer or small knife and cover with screw-top lids. Label and leave to mature in a cool, dark place for at least 3 weeks.

Ale, Apple &
Mustard Chutney

MAKES 4 jars
PREPARATION TIME 30 minutes
COOKING TIME 1¾–2 hours

1 kg (2 lb) cooking apples, peeled, cored, quartered and diced
500 g (1 lb) onions, finely chopped
250 g (8 oz) celery, diced
250 g (8 oz) stoned dates, diced
550 ml (1 pint) brown ale
150 ml (¼ pint) malt vinegar
300 g (10 oz) demerara sugar
2 tablespoons white mustard seeds, roughly crushed
1 teaspoon turmeric
1 teaspoon salt
1 teaspoon peppercorns, roughly crushed

Add all the ingredients to a preserving pan and cook, uncovered, over a gentle heat for 1¾–2 hours, stirring from time to time, but more frequently towards the end of cooking as the chutney thickens.

Ladle into warm, dry jars, filling to the very top and pressing down well. Disperse any air pockets with a skewer or small knife and cover with screw-top lids. Label and leave to mature in a cool, dark place for at least 3 weeks.

Serve this chutney as part of a ploughman's lunch.

Apple &
Tomato Chutney

MAKES 6 jars
PREPARATION TIME 30 minutes
COOKING TIME 1½ hours

1 kg (2 lb) mixed green and red tomatoes, roughly chopped
500 g (1 lb) cooking apples, peeled, cored and diced
1 marrow (about 750 g / 1½ lb), peeled, halved, deseeded and diced
500 g (1 lb) onions, roughly chopped
100 g (3½ oz) sultanas or raisins
300 ml (½ pint) distilled malt vinegar
250 g (8 oz) granulated sugar
1 tablespoon tomato purée
2 teaspoons hot paprika
2 teaspoons English mustard powder
1 teaspoon salt
2 teaspoons peppercorns, roughly crushed

Add all the ingredients to a preserving pan, stir to combine, then cook, uncovered, over a gentle heat for 1½ hours, stirring from time to time, but more frequently towards the end of cooking as the chutney thickens.

Ladle into warm, dry jars, filling to the very top and pressing down well. Disperse any air pockets with a skewer or small knife and cover with screw-top lids. Label and leave to mature in a cool, dark place for at least 3 weeks.

Runner Bean Chutney

MAKES 6 jars
PREPARATION TIME 25 minutes
COOKING TIME about 35 minutes

1 kg (2 lb) runner beans, trimmed
900 ml (1½ pints) distilled malt vinegar
750 g (1½ lb) demerara sugar
500 g (1 lb) onions, chopped
1½ tablespoons turmeric

1½ tablespoons mustard powder
3 tablespoons black mustard seeds
3 tablespoons cornflour
1 teaspoon salt
a little pepper
3 tablespoons water

Half-fill a preserving pan with water, bring to the boil, then add the runner beans. Return to the boil and cook for 3 minutes. Drain into a colander, refresh with cold water, then drain again. Thinly slice the beans or roughly chop in a food processor.

Add the vinegar and sugar to the drained preserving pan, then add the onions. Cover and bring to the boil, then reduce the heat and simmer for 10 minutes.

Mix the remaining dry ingredients together in a bowl, then stir in the measurement water until smooth. Stir this into the vinegar mixture, then simmer, uncovered, for 10 minutes, stirring until smooth and thickened.

Stir the blanched beans into the vinegar mixture and cook gently for 10 minutes, stirring frequently until just tender. Ladle into warm, dry jars, pressing the beans down well in the vinegar mix. Disperse any air pockets with a skewer or small knife and cover with screw-top lids. Label and leave to mature in a cool, dark place for at least 3 weeks.

Pumpkin & Red Pepper Chutney

MAKES 3 jars
PREPARATION TIME 30 minutes
COOKING TIME 1¼ hours

1 kg (2 lb) pumpkin, weighed after peeling and deseeding, sliced

2 red peppers, quartered, deseeded and cored

500 g (1 lb) shallots, halved if large

3 bay leaves

3 tablespoons olive oil

400 ml (14 fl oz) cider vinegar or white wine vinegar

125 g (4 oz) granulated sugar

125 g (4 oz) light muscovado sugar

1 teaspoon allspice berries, roughly crushed

½ teaspoon salt

½ teaspoon cayenne pepper

Add the pumpkin, red peppers and shallots to a large roasting tin. Tuck the bay leaves in among the vegetables, then drizzle with the oil. Roast in a preheated oven, 200°C (400°F), Gas Mark 6, for 45 minutes until the vegetables are tender and browned.

Leave to cool slightly, then remove the skins from the peppers. Roughly chop the peppers, pumpkin and shallots, discarding the bay leaves. Add the vegetables and any juices from the roasting tin to a preserving pan. Add all the remaining ingredients, then bring to the boil and simmer, uncovered, for about 30 minutes, stirring more frequently towards the end of cooking, until thick.

Ladle into warm, dry jars, filling to the very top and pressing down well. Disperse any air pockets with a skewer or small knife and cover with screw-top lids. Label and leave to mature in a cool, dark place for at least 3 weeks.

Pumpkin & Walnut Chutney

MAKES 4 jars
PREPARATION TIME 30 minutes
COOKING TIME 1½–2 hours

1 kg (2 lb) pumpkin, weighed after peeling and deseeding, diced
2 onions, finely chopped
1 large orange, finely chopped, including pith and peel
600 ml (1 pint) white wine vinegar
375 g (12 oz) granulated sugar
1 cinnamon stick, halved
5 cm (2 inch) piece root ginger, peeled and finely chopped
1 teaspoon turmeric
1 teaspoon dried crushed red chillies
1 teaspoon salt
a little pepper
50 g (2 oz) walnut pieces

Add the pumpkin to a preserving pan with all the remaining ingredients. Cover and cook gently for 1 hour, stirring from time to time, until softened. Remove the lid and cook for 30 minutes–1 hour, stirring more frequently towards the end of cooking as the chutney thickens.

Ladle into warm, dry jars, filling to the very top and pressing down well. Disperse any air pockets with a skewer or small knife and cover with screw-top lids. Label and leave to mature in a cool, dark place for at least 3 weeks.

Pumpkin &
Date Chutney

MAKES 4 jars
PREPARATION TIME 30 minutes
COOKING TIME 1½–2 hours

1 kg (2 lb) pumpkin, weighed after peeling and deseeding, diced
2 onions, finely chopped
1 large orange, finely chopped, including pith and peel
600 ml (1 pint) white wine vinegar
375 g (12 oz) granulated sugar
1 cinnamon stick, halved
5 cm (2 inch) piece root ginger, peeled and finely chopped
1 teaspoon turmeric
1 teaspoon dried crushed red chillies
1 teaspoon salt
a little pepper
25 g (4 oz) stoned dates, diced

Add the pumpkin to a preserving pan with all the remaining ingredients. Cover and cook gently for 1 hour, stirring from time to time, until softened. Remove the lid and cook for 30 minutes–1 hour, stirring more frequently towards the end of cooking as the chutney thickens.

Ladle into warm, dry jars, filling to the very top and pressing down well. Disperse any air pockets with a skewer or small knife and cover with screw-top lids. Label and leave to mature in a cool, dark place for at least 3 weeks.

Roasted Root Chutney

MAKES 3 jars
PREPARATION TIME 30 minutes
COOKING TIME 1¼ hours

500 g (1 lb) parsnips, peeled and sliced
500 g (1 lb) sweet potato, peeled and sliced
2 red peppers, quartered, deseeded and cored
500 g (1 lb) shallots, halved if large
3 bay leaves
3 tablespoons olive oil

400 ml (14 fl oz) cider vinegar or white wine vinegar
125 g (4 oz) granulated sugar
125 g (4 oz) light muscovado sugar
1 teaspoon turmeric
1 teaspoon smoked paprika
½ teaspoon salt
½ teaspoon cayenne pepper

Add the parsnips, sweet potato, red peppers and shallots to a large roasting tin. Tuck the bay leaves in among the vegetables, then drizzle with the oil. Roast in a preheated oven, 200°C (400°F), Gas Mark 6, for 45 minutes until the vegetables are tender and browned.

Leave to cool slightly, then remove the skins from the peppers. Roughly chop the parsnips, sweet potato, peppers and shallots, discarding the bay leaves. Add the vegetables and any juices from the roasting to a preserving pan. Add all the remaining ingredients, then bring to the boil and simmer, uncovered, for about 30 minutes, stirring more frequently towards the end of cooking, until thick.

Ladle into warm, dry jars, filling to the very top and pressing down well. Disperse any air pockets with a skewer or small knife and cover with screw-top lids. Label and leave to mature in a cool, dark place for at least 3 weeks.

Mango & Black
Onion Seed Chutney

MAKES 3 jars
PREPARATION TIME 30 minutes
COOKING TIME 20 minutes

300 ml (½ pint) distilled
malt vinegar
375 g (12 oz) granulated sugar
2 garlic cloves, finely chopped
5 cm (2 inch) piece root ginger,
peeled and finely chopped
4 dried chillies, finely chopped
½ teaspoon ground allspice

2 tablespoons black
onion seeds
1 teaspoon salt
1 teaspoon mixed
peppercorns, roughly
crushed
4 large, firm, unripe mangoes,
peeled and stoned

Add the vinegar, sugar, garlic and ginger to a preserving pan, then add the dried chillies, allspice, black onion seeds, salt and peppercorns. Heat gently, stirring from time to time, until the sugar has dissolved, then simmer gently for 10 minutes so that the flavours mingle together.

Meanwhile, finely chop 2 of the mangoes and slice the remaining 2.

Stir in the mangoes and cook over a medium heat for 10 minutes until they are just translucent and the liquid is syrupy.

Ladle into warm, dry jars, filling to the very top. Press the mango slices beneath the syrup, then cover with screw-top lids. Label and leave to mature in a cool, dark place for at least 3 weeks.

To serve, partner with poppadums.

Mango &
Pineapple Chutney

MAKES 3 jars
PREPARATION TIME 30 minutes
COOKING TIME 20 minutes

300 ml (½ pint) distilled
   malt vinegar
375 g (12 oz) granulated sugar
2 garlic cloves, finely chopped
5 cm (2 inch) piece root ginger,
   peeled and finely chopped
4 dried chillies, finely chopped
½ teaspoon ground allspice
1 teaspoon salt

1 teaspoon mixed
   peppercorns, roughly
   crushed
1 large pineapple, trimmed,
   peeled, cored and finely
   chopped in a food
   processor
2 large, firm, unripe mangoes,
   peeled, stoned and sliced

Add the vinegar, sugar, garlic and ginger to a preserving pan, then add the dried chillies, allspice, salt and peppercorns. Heat gently, stirring from time to time, until the sugar has dissolved, then simmer gently for 10 minutes so that the flavours mingle together.

Stir in the pineapple and mangoes and cook over a medium heat for 10 minutes until the mango is just translucent and the liquid is syrupy.

Ladle into warm, dry jars, filling to the very top. Press the mango slices beneath the syrup, then cover with screw-top lids. Label and leave to mature in a cool, dark place for at least 3 weeks.

To serve, partner with poppadums.

Mango, Apple
& Mint Chutney

SERVES 4–6
PREPARATION TIME 10 minutes

1 green mango, peeled, stoned
    and roughly chopped
1 small apple, peeled, cored
    and roughly chopped
1 teaspoon salt

1 tablespoon chopped
    mint leaves
1 teaspoon mild chilli powder
1 teaspoon soft brown sugar
150 ml (¼ pint) water

Put all the ingredients into a food processor or blender and process until smooth.

Transfer the mixture to a small serving dish, cover and chill until required. The chutney will keep for up to 3 days in the refrigerator.

Red Onion & Raisin Chutney

MAKES 1 jar
PREPARATION TIME 15 minutes
COOKING TIME 1 hour 25 minutes–1 hour 30 minutes

3 tablespoons olive oil
1.5 kg (3 lb) red onions,
    thinly sliced
225 g (8 oz) light muscovado
    sugar
300 ml (½ pint) red wine
    vinegar

200 g (7 oz) raisins
3 garlic cloves, chopped
3 bay leaves
1 tablespoon wholegrain
    mustard
salt and pepper

Heat the oil in a large saucepan and fry the onions over a medium heat for 10 minutes until softened.

Stir in 25 g (1 oz) of the sugar, fry gently for 15 minutes until browned, then stir in remaining sugar, the vinegar, raisins, garlic, bay leaves, mustard, salt and pepper. Simmer gently for 30 minutes, stirring from time to time, until the chutney has thickened.

Ladle into a warm, dry jar. Disperse any air pockets with a skewer or small knife and cover with a screw-top lid. Label and leave to mature in a cool, dark place for at least 3 weeks.

Peach &
Date Chutney

MAKES 3–4 jars
PREPARATION TIME 10 minutes
COOKING TIME 50 minutes

12 peaches
500 g (1 lb) onions, finely
    chopped
2 garlic cloves, crushed
2 tablespoons grated
    root ginger

125 g (4 oz) stoned dates,
    chopped
250 g (8 oz) demerara sugar
300 ml (½ pint) red wine
    vinegar
salt and pepper

Place the peaches in a large bowl, cover with boiling water
and leave to stand for about 1 minute, then drain and peel.
Halve and stone the peaches and cut into thick slices.

Add the onions to a sauce pan with the peaches, garlic,
ginger, dates, sugar and vinegar. Add a generous sprinkling
of salt and pepper and bring to the boil, stirring
continuously, until the sugar has completely dissolved.

Reduce the heat and simmer, covered, stirring frequently,
for 45 minutes, until the chutney has thickened.

Ladle into warm, dry jars. Disperse any air pockets with
a skewer or small knife and cover with screw-top lids. Label
and leave to mature in a cool, dark place for at least 3 weeks.

Tamarind & Date Chutney

SERVES 4
PREPARATION TIME 10 minutes

200 g (7 oz) stoned dates,
roughly chopped
1 tablespoon tamarind paste
1 teaspoon ground cumin

1 teaspoon chilli powder
1 tablespoon tomato ketchup
200 ml (7 fl oz) water
salt

Put all the ingredients into a food processor or blender and process until fairly smooth.

Transfer the mixture to a serving bowl, cover and chill until required. The chutney will keep for up to 3 days in the refrigerator.

Garlicky Mediterranean Chutney

MAKES 3 jars
PREPARATION TIME 20 minutes
COOKING TIME 1½ hours

4 garlic cloves, finely chopped
300 g (10 oz) onions, chopped
500 g (1 lb) tomatoes, skinned (optional) and roughly chopped
375 g (12 oz) courgettes, diced
4 peppers of different colours, deseeded, cored and diced
1 aubergine, diced
250 ml (8 fl oz) red wine vinegar
250 g (8 oz) granulated sugar
1 tablespoon tomato purée
3 sprigs rosemary, leaves chopped
salt and pepper

Add all the ingredients to a preserving pan and cook, uncovered, over a gentle heat for 1½ hours, stirring from time to time, but more frequently towards the end of cooking as the chutney thickens.

Ladle into warm, dry jars, filling to the very top and pressing down well. Disperse any air pockets with a skewer or small knife and cover with screw-top lids. Label and leave to mature in a cool, dark place for at least 3 weeks.

Christmas Plum Chutney

MAKES 3 jars
PREPARATION TIME 30 minutes
COOKING TIME 1¼–1½ hours

500 g (1 lb) plums, stoned
  and sliced
500 g (1 lb) red onions,
  thinly sliced
250 g (8 oz) mixed dried fruit
250 g (8 oz) light muscovado
  sugar

300 ml (½ pint) red wine
  vinegar
2 teaspoons ground
  mixed spice
1 teaspoon dried crushed
  chillies
1 teaspoon salt
½ teaspoon pepper

Add all the ingredients to a preserving pan, cover and
simmer gently for 1 hour, stirring from time to time,
until softened.

Remove the lid and cook for 15–30 minutes until thick,
stirring more frequently towards the end of cooking, until
the plums are very soft and the chutney is thick.

Spoon into warm, dry jars, filling to the very top and
pressing down well. Disperse any air pockets with a
skewer or small knife and cover with screw-top lids. Label
and leave to mature in a cool, dark place for at least 3 weeks.

Smooth Plum & Tomato Chutney

MAKES 2 jars
PREPARATION TIME 25 minutes
COOKING TIME 1 hour

½ teaspoon cumin seeds
½ teaspoon fennel seeds
1 teaspoon coriander seeds
½ teaspoon dried chilli flakes
500 g (1 lb) plums, stoned and diced
500 g (1 lb) tomatoes, roughly chopped
1 onion, chopped
2.5 cm (1 inch) piece root ginger, peeled and finely chopped
150 ml (¼ pint) malt vinegar
125 g (4 oz) granulated sugar
2 tablespoons raisins
juice of 1 lemon
salt and pepper

Crush the seeds roughly in a pestle and mortar, then toast in a hot preserving pan with the chilli flakes for a few seconds. Add all the remaining ingredients, then cover and simmer gently for 30 minutes, stirring from time to time.

Uncover the chutney and cook for 30 minutes, stirring until thick and pulpy. Mash with a potato masher, or blitz in a food processor or blender, until smooth.

Ladle into warm, dry jars, filling to the very top and pressing down well. Disperse any air pockets with a skewer or small knife and cover with screw-top lids. Label and leave to mature in a cool, dark place for at least 3 weeks.

To serve, try adding to a cheese and salad sandwich.

Peach & Orange Chutney

MAKES 3–4 jars
PREPARATION TIME 10 minutes
COOKING TIME 50 minutes

12 peaches
500 g (1 lb) onions, finely
    chopped
1 orange, finely chopped
2 tablespoons grated root
    ginger
125 g (4 oz) stoned dates,
    chopped

125 g (4 oz) carrot, coarsely
    grated
2 garlic cloves, crushed
250 g (8 oz) demerara sugar
300 ml (½ pint) white wine
    vinegar
salt and pepper

Place the peaches in a large bowl, cover with boiling water
and leave to stand for 1 minute, then drain and peel. Halve
and stone the peaches and cut into thick slices.

Add the onions to a pan with the peaches, orange, ginger,
dates, carrot, garlic, sugar and vinegar. Add a generous
sprinkling of salt and pepper and bring to the boil, stirring
continuously, until the sugar has completely dissolved.

Reduce the heat and simmer, covered, stirring frequently,
for 45 minutes, until the chutney has thickened.

Ladle into warm, dry jars. Disperse any air pockets with
a skewer or small knife and cover with screw-top lids. Label
and leave to mature in a cool, dark place for at least 3 weeks.

Apple, Marrow & Ginger Jam

MAKES 6 jars
PREPARATION TIME 25 minutes
COOKING TIME 35–40 minutes

1.75 kg (3½ lb) cooking apples, cored, quartered and diced

1 small marrow, 750–875 g (1½–1¾ lb), peeled, deseeded and diced

100 g (3½ oz) stem ginger, drained and finely chopped

grated rind and juice of 2 lemons

300 ml (½ pint) water

1.5 kg (3 lb) granulated sugar, warmed

15 g (½ oz) butter (optional)

Add the apples, marrow, stem ginger and the grated rind and lemon juice to a preserving pan with the measured water, then cover and cook for 20 minutes, until just tender.

Pour the sugar into the pan and heat gently, stirring from time to time, until dissolved. Bring to the boil, then boil rapidly until setting point is reached (15–20 minutes).

Skim with a draining spoon or stir in the butter if needed.

Ladle into warm, dry jars, filling to the very top. Cover with screw-top lids, or with waxed discs and cellophane tops secured with elastic bands. Label and leave to mature in a cool, dark place for at least 3 weeks.

To serve, this jam is delicious simply eaten with bread and butter.

All-American Tomato Relish

MAKES 2 jars
PREPARATION TIME 20 minutes
COOKING TIME 1 hour 5 minutes

2 tablespoons sunflower oil
2 onions, roughly chopped
2 Granny Smith apples,
  peeled, cored, quartered
  and diced
1 kg (2 lb) tomatoes, skinned
  and roughly chopped
250 g (8 oz) granulated sugar

2 tablespoons tomato purée
300 ml (½ pint) distilled
  malt vinegar
1 tablespoon Worcestershire
  sauce
1 teaspoon paprika
2 bay leaves
salt and pepper

Heat the oil in a saucepan, add the onions and fry for
5 minutes until softened. Add the apples and tomatoes,
then stir in the remaining ingredients.

Cook over a gentle heat, uncovered, for about 1 hour,
stirring more frequently towards the end of cooking as the
relish thickens.

Ladle into warm, dry jars, pressing down well and filling
to the top. Disperse any air pockets with a skewer or small
knife and cover with screw-top lids. Label and leave to
mature in a cool, dark place for at least 3 weeks.

To serve, this relish is perfect for dipping chips.

Chillied Tomato Relish

MAKES 3 jars
PREPARATION TIME 25 minutes
COOKING TIME 1 hour 5 minutes

2 tablespoons sunflower oil
500 g (1 lb) onions, finely
   chopped
1 kg (2 lb) tomatoes, skinned
   (optional) and roughly
   chopped
4 red finger chillies, deseeded
   and chopped

3 sprigs thyme
2 tablespoons tomato purée
1 teaspoon smoked paprika
300 ml (½ pint) distilled
   malt vinegar
250 g (8 oz) granulated sugar
salt and pepper

Heat the oil in a preserving pan, add the onions and fry for 5 minutes until softened. Stir in the tomatoes and chillies, then add the remaining ingredients.

Cook, uncovered, for 1 hour, stirring more frequently towards the end of cooking as the relish thickens.

Ladle into warm, dry jars, pressing down well and filling to the top. Disperse any air pockets with a skewer or small knife and cover with screw-top lids. Label and leave to mature in a cool, dark place for at least 3 weeks.

To serve, this relish goes well with Chinese-style pancake rolls, prawn sesame toast and bite-sized dumplings.

Garlicky Tomato Relish

MAKES 2 jars
PREPARATION TIME 20 minutes
COOKING TIME 1 hour 5 minutes

2 tablespoons sunflower oil
2 onions, roughly chopped
2 Granny Smith apples,
    peeled, cored, quartered
    and diced
1 kg (2 lb) tomatoes, skinned
    and roughly chopped
4 garlic cloves, finely chopped

300 ml (½ pint) distilled
    malt vinegar
250 g (8 oz) granulated sugar
2 tablespoons tomato purée
1 tablespoon Worcestershire
    sauce
1 teaspoon paprika
2 bay leaves
salt and pepper

Heat the oil in a saucepan, add the onions and fry for
5 minutes until softened. Add the apples, tomatoes and
garlic, then stir in the remaining ingredients.

Cook over a gentle heat, uncovered, for 1 hour,
stirring more frequently towards the end of cooking as
the relish thickens.

Ladle into warm, dry jars, pressing down well and filling
to the top. Disperse any air pockets with a skewer or small
knife and cover with screw-top lids. Label and leave to
mature in a cool, dark place for at least 3 weeks.

To serve, this relish is perfect for dipping chunky chips.

Jerked Tomato Relish

MAKES 3 jars
PREPARATION TIME 25 minutes
COOKING TIME 1 hour 5 minutes

2 tablespoons sunflower oil
500 g (1 lb) onions, finely chopped
1 kg (2 lb) tomatoes, skinned (optional) and roughly chopped
4 red finger chillies, deseeded and chopped
3 sprigs thyme
2 tablespoons tomato purée
1 teaspoon smoked paprika
1 teaspoon allspice berries, crushed
1 teaspoon black peppercorns, crushed
½ teaspoon ground cinnamon
2 garlic cloves, finely chopped
grated rind and juice of 1 lime
300 ml (½ pint) distilled malt vinegar
250 g (8 oz) granulated sugar
salt and pepper

Heat the oil in a preserving pan, add the onions and fry for 5 minutes until softened. Stir in the tomatoes and chillies, then add the remaining ingredients.

Cook, uncovered, for 1 hour, stirring more frequently towards the end of cooking as the relish thickens.

Ladle into warm, dry jars, pressing down well and filling to the top. Disperse any air pockets with a skewer or small knife and cover with screw-top lids. Label and leave to mature in a cool, dark place for at least 3 weeks.

To serve, this relish goes well with grilled and roasted meats and seafood.

Tomato & Aubergine Relish

MAKES 4 jars
PREPARATION TIME 20 minutes
COOKING TIME about 30 minutes

1 kg (2 lb) ripe tomatoes, skinned and chopped
1 kg (2 lb) aubergines, finely diced
500 g (1 lb) onions, finely chopped
2 red chillies, deseeded and finely chopped
2 tablespoons tomato purée
450 ml (¾ pint) red wine vinegar
175 g (6 oz) soft light brown sugar
4 tablespoons mustard seeds
2 tablespoons celery seeds
1 tablespoon paprika
2 teaspoons salt
2 teaspoons pepper

Combine all the ingredients in a large saucepan.

Bring the mixture to the boil over a moderate heat, then reduce the heat and simmer, uncovered, for about 30 minutes until most of the liquid has evaporated and the relish has a thick, pulpy consistency. Stir frequently as the relish thickens.

Ladle into warm, dry jars. Disperse any air pockets with a skewer or small knife and cover with screw-top lids. Label and leave to mature in a cool, dark place for at least 3 weeks.

Tomato & Pepper Relish

MAKES 4 jars
PREPARATION TIME 20 minutes
COOKING TIME about 30 minutes

1 kg (2 lb) ripe tomatoes, skinned and chopped
1 kg (2 lb) red peppers, deseeded, cored and finely chopped
500 g (1 lb) onions, finely chopped
2 red chillies, deseeded and finely chopped

450 ml (¾ pint) red wine vinegar
175 g (6 oz) soft light brown sugar
4 tablespoons mustard seeds
2 tablespoons celery seeds
1 tablespoon paprika
2 teaspoons salt
2 teaspoons pepper

Combine all the ingredients in a large saucepan.

Bring the mixture to the boil over a moderate heat, then reduce the heat and simmer, uncovered, for about 30 minutes until most of the liquid has evaporated and the relish has a thick, pulpy consistency. Stir frequently as the relish thickens.

Ladle into warm, dry jars. Disperse any air pockets with a skewer or small knife and cover with screw-top lids. Label and leave to mature in a cool, dark place for at least 3 weeks.

Cucumber & Pepper Relish

MAKES 3 jars
PREPARATION TIME 30 minutes + soaking
COOKING TIME 25 minutes

2 cucumbers, diced
50 g (2 oz) salt
1 tablespoon sunflower oil
2 onions, chopped
2 red peppers, cored,
  deseeded and diced
300 ml (½ pint) distilled
  malt vinegar
300 g (10 oz) granulated sugar

1 teaspoon dried crushed
  red chillies
½ teaspoon turmeric
2 teaspoons mustard powder
2 tablespoons cornflour
2 tablespoons water
½ teaspoon peppercorns,
  roughly crushed

Layer the cucumbers in a bowl with the salt, cover with a plate, weigh down and set aside for 4 hours. Tip into a colander, drain off the liquid, then rinse with cold water and drain well.

Heat the oil in a preserving pan, add the onions and fry for 5 minutes, stirring until softened. Add the red peppers and fry for a further 5 minutes.

Add the vinegar and sugar to the pan. Mix the chillies, turmeric, mustard powder and cornflour in a bowl, then stir in the measurement water and mix until smooth. Stir this into the vinegar mixture and mix until smooth.

Cook gently for 10 minutes, stirring from time to time, until thickened. Stir in the cucumber and peppercorns and cook for 5 minutes.

Ladle into warm, dry jars, pressing down well and making sure that the vinegar mixture covers the vegetables.

Disperse any air pockets with a skewer or small knife and cover with screw-top lids. Label and leave to mature in a cool, dark place for at least 3 weeks.

Mixed Pepper Relish

MAKES 3 jars
PREPARATION TIME 30 minutes + soaking
COOKING TIME 25 minutes

1 tablespoon sunflower oil
1 onion, chopped
2 red peppers, cored,
   deseeded and diced
2 orange peppers, cored,
   deseeded and diced
2 green peppers, cored,
   deseeded and diced
300 ml (½ pint) distilled
   malt vinegar

300 g (10 oz) granulated sugar
1 teaspoon dried crushed
   red chillies
½ teaspoon turmeric
2 teaspoons mustard powder
2 tablespoons cornflour
2 tablespoons water
½ teaspoon peppercorns,
   roughly crushed

Heat the oil in a preserving pan, add the onion and fry for 5 minutes, stirring until softened. Add the peppers and fry for a further 5 minutes.

Add the vinegar and sugar to the pan. Mix the chillies, turmeric, mustard powder and cornflour in a bowl, then stir in the measurement water and mix until smooth. Stir this into the vinegar mixture and mix until smooth. Cook gently for 10 minutes, stirring from time to time, until thickened. Stir in the peppercorns and cook for 5 minutes.

Ladle into warm, dry jars, pressing down well and making sure that the vinegar mixture covers the vegetables.

Disperse any air pockets with a skewer or small knife and cover with screw-top lids. Label and leave to mature in a cool, dark place for at least 3 weeks.

Sweet Chilli & Kaffir Lime Relish

MAKES 2 jars
PREPARATION TIME 25 minutes
COOKING TIME 1 hour

500 g (1 lb) onions, finely
  chopped
4 limes, finely chopped
  including pith and peel
6 green finger chillies,
  including seeds, chopped
2 green peppers, cored,
  deseeded and diced

1 tablespoon black
  mustard seeds
1 teaspoon turmeric
4 kaffir lime leaves
300 ml (½ pint) distilled
  malt vinegar
500 g (1 lb) granulated sugar
1 teaspoon salt
a little pepper

Add all the ingredients to a preserving pan, cover and simmer gently for 45 minutes, stirring from time to time.

Remove the lid and cook for a further 15 minutes until the limes are soft, stirring more frequently towards the end of cooking as the relish thickens.

Ladle into warm, dry jars, pressing down well and filling to the top. Disperse any air pockets with a skewer or small knife and cover with screw-top lids. Label and leave to mature for at least 3 weeks.

Lime
Pickle

MAKES 1 jar
PREPARATION TIME 20 minutes + maturing
COOKING TIME 5 minutes

10 limes, each cut
   into 6 segments
100 g (3½ oz) salt
1 tablespoon fenugreek seeds
1 tablespoon black
   mustard seeds

1 tablespoon chilli powder
1 tablespoon ground turmeric
300 ml (½ pint) vegetable oil
½ teaspoon asafoetida

Put the limes into a sterilized jar and cover with the salt.
Dry-fry the fenugreek and mustard seeds in a small frying
pan, and then grind them to a powder. Add the ground
seeds, chilli powder and turmeric to the limes and mix well.

Heat the oil in a small frying pan until smoking, add the
asafoetida and fry for 30 seconds. Pour the flavoured oil over
the limes and mix well.

Cover the jar with a clean cloth and leave to mature for
10 days in a bright, warm place.

Transfer the pickle to an airtight container and store for
up to 2 months.

Spiced Peach Relish

MAKES 2 jars
PREPARATION TIME 25 minutes
COOKING TIME 45 minutes

1 kg (2 lb) peaches, stoned and finely diced
2 onions, chopped
10 cardamom pods, crushed
1 cinnamon stick
4 cloves
300 ml (½ pint) distilled malt vinegar
250 g (8 oz) granulated sugar
1 teaspoon salt
a little pepper

Add all the ingredients to a preserving pan.

Cook gently, uncovered, for 45 minutes until the peaches are soft, stirring from time to time, but more frequently towards the end of cooking as the relish thickens.

Ladle into warm, dry jars, pressing down well and filling to the top. Disperse any air pockets with a skewer or small knife and cover with screw-top lids. Label and leave to mature in a cool, dark place for at least 3 weeks.

To serve, this relish is very tasty with pork pie, little gem lettuce leaves and spring onions.

South Seas Relish

MAKES 2 jars
PREPARATION TIME 25 minutes
COOKING TIME 1 hour

250 g (8 oz) onions, finely
  chopped
250 g (8 oz) fresh pineapple,
  finely chopped
4 limes, chopped including
  pith and peel
6 green finger chillies,
  including seeds, finely
  chopped
1 red pepper, cored, deseeded
  and finely chopped

1 green pepper, cored,
  deseeded and finely
  chopped
1 teaspoon allspice berries,
  roughly crushed
1 teaspoon turmeric
300 ml (½ pint) distilled
  malt vinegar
500 g (1 lb) granulated sugar
1 teaspoon salt
a little pepper

Add all the ingredients to a preserving pan, cover and simmer gently for 45 minutes, stirring from time to time.

Remove the lid and cook for a further 15 minutes until the limes are soft, stirring more frequently towards the end of cooking as the relish thickens.

Ladle into warm, dry jars, pressing down well and filling the jars to the tops. Disperse any air pockets with a skewer or small knife and cover with screw-top lids. Label and leave to mature for at least 3 weeks.

Piccalilli

MAKES 2–3 jars
PREPARATION TIME 10 minutes + standing
COOKING TIME 25 minutes

1 small cauliflower, cut into small florets, large stalks discarded
½ cucumber, peeled and roughly chopped
2 onions, chopped
2 large carrots (about 50 g/ 2 oz), peeled and cut into chunks

salt
2 tablespoons plain flour
300 ml (½ pint) cider vinegar
250 g (8 oz) granulated sugar
½ teaspoon ground turmeric
½ teaspoon ground ginger
2 teaspoons mustard powder
a little pepper

Layer the vegetables in a large bowl, sprinkling each layer with the salt, then cover and leave to stand overnight. The next day, lightly rinse and thoroughly dry the vegetables.

Mix the flour to a smooth paste with a little of the vinegar. Heat the remaining vinegar in a large saucepan with the sugar, spices and mustard powder over a low heat, stirring continuously, until the sugar has dissolved. Increase the heat and bring to the boil, then season the mixture generously with pepper and add the vegetables. Bring back to the boil, then reduce the heat and simmer, uncovered, for 10 minutes.

Remove the pan from the heat and gradually stir in the flour mixture. Return to the heat, bring to the boil and simmer for a further 5 minutes.

Ladle into warm, dry jars. Disperse any air pockets with a skewer or small knife and cover with screw-top lids. Label and leave to mature in a cool, dark place for at least 3 weeks.

To serve, partner with slivers of Parma ham.

Three-Bean Mustard Pickle

MAKES 4 jars
PREPARATION TIME 25 minutes
COOKING TIME 23 minutes

250 g (8 oz) podded broad
 beans
250 g (8 oz) French beans,
 each cut into three
250 g (8 oz) runner beans,
 thinly sliced
500 ml cider vinegar or white
 wine vinegar
375 g (12 oz) caster sugar
2 medium onions, chopped
3 garlic cloves, finely chopped

2 tablespoons cornflour
1 tablespoon turmeric
1 tablespoon mustard powder
1 tablespoon wholegrain
 mustard
2 teaspoons fennel seeds,
 roughly crushed
1 teaspoon salt
a little pepper
2 tablespoons water

Bring a large saucepan of water to the boil. Add the beans, cover and bring back to the boil, then cook for 3 minutes. Drain and refresh with cold water, then drain again.

Pour the vinegar and sugar into a preserving pan, add the onions and garlic, then cover and bring to the boil. Reduce the heat and simmer for 10 minutes.

Mix the remaining dry ingredients together in a bowl, then mix to a smooth paste with the measurement water. Stir into the vinegar mixture and cook, uncovered, for 5 minutes, stirring until slightly thickened.

Add the blanched vegetables, cook for a further 5 minutes, stirring, until the vegetables are just tender, then ladle into warm, dry jars, pressing the vegetables down below the liquid with a fork and making sure there are no air pockets. Label and leave to mature in a cool, dark place for 3–4 weeks.

Something Different

Apple & Ginger Beer Chutney

MAKES 4 jars
PREPARATION TIME 30 minutes
COOKING TIME 1¾–2 hours

1 kg (2 lb) cooking apples, peeled, cored, quartered and diced
500 g (1 lb) onions, finely chopped
250 g (8 oz) celery, diced
250 g (8 oz) sultanas
550 ml ginger beer

150 ml (¼ pint) malt vinegar
300 g (10 oz) demerara sugar
2 tablespoons white mustard seeds, roughly crushed
1 teaspoon turmeric
1 teaspoon salt
1 teaspoon peppercorns, roughly crushed

Add all the ingredients to a preserving pan and cook, uncovered, over a gentle heat for 1¾–2 hours, stirring from time to time, but more frequently towards the end of cooking as the chutney thickens.

Ladle into warm, dry jars, filling to the very top and pressing down well. Disperse any air pockets with a skewer or small knife and cover with screw-top lids. Label and leave to mature in a cool, dark place for at least 3 weeks.

To serve, this chutney is delicious as part of a ploughman's lunch.

Bloody Mary Jelly

MAKES 4 jars
PREPARATION TIME 30 minutes + straining
COOKING TIME 1 hour 20 minutes–1 hour 30 minutes

250 g (8 oz) red onions, roughly chopped
125 g (4 oz) celery, roughly chopped
1 kg (2 lb) tomatoes, roughly chopped (not skinned or deseeded)
500 g (1 lb) windfall cooking apples, any bruised areas cut away, roughly chopped (not peeled or cored)
600 ml (1 pint) water

200 ml (7 fl oz) red wine vinegar
about 1.25 kg (2½ lb) granulated sugar
1 tablespoon tomato purée
juice of 2 lemons
15 g (½ oz) butter (optional)
50 g (2 oz) sun-blush tomatoes in oil, drained and diced
4 tablespoons vodka (optional)

Add the onions, celery, tomatoes and apples to a preserving pan. Pour in the measurement water and vinegar, then bring to the boil. Reduce the heat, cover and simmer gently for 1 hour, stirring and mashing from time to time with a fork, until the tomatoes and apples are pulpy.

Allow to cool slightly, pour into a scalded jelly bag suspended over a large bowl and allow to drip for several hours.

Measure the clear liquid and then pour back into the rinsed preserving pan. Weigh 500 g (1 lb) sugar for every 600 ml (1 pint) of liquid, then pour into the preserving pan. Add the tomato purée and lemon juice and heat gently, stirring from time to time, until the sugar has dissolved.

Bring to the boil, then boil rapidly until setting point is reached (20–30 minutes).

Skim with a draining spoon or stir in the butter if needed. Stir in the sun-blush tomatoes and vodka, if liked, and leave to stand for 15 minutes so that the tomatoes don't rise in the jelly when potted. Ladle into warm, dry jars, filling to the very top. Cover with screw-top lids, or with waxed discs and cellophane tops secured with elastic bands. Label and leave to cool.

To serve, this jelly goes well with cold meats, such as salami and Parma ham, olives and sun-blush tomatoes.

Caribbean Vegetable Pickle

MAKES 2–3 jars
PREPARATION TIME 10 minutes + standing
COOKING TIME 25 minutes

½ cauliflower, cut into small florets, large stalks discarded
1 large aubergine cut into cubes
½ small butternut squash, peeled, deseeded and cubed
100 g (3½ oz) green beans, cut into 2.5 cm (1 inch) lengths

1 onion, chopped
50 g (2 oz) salt
2 tablespoons plain flour
300 ml (½ pint) cider vinegar
250 g (8 oz) granulated sugar
½ teaspoon ground turmeric
½ teaspoon ground ginger
2 teaspoons mustard powder
a little pepper

Layer the vegetables in a large bowl, sprinkling each layer with the salt, then cover and leave to stand overnight. The next day, lightly rinse and thoroughly dry the vegetables.

Mix the flour to a smooth paste with a little of the vinegar. Heat the remaining vinegar in a large saucepan with the sugar, spices and mustard powder over a low heat, stirring continuously, until the sugar has dissolved. Increase the heat and bring to the boil, then season the mixture generously with pepper and add the vegetables. Bring back to the boil, then reduce the heat and simmer, uncovered, for 10 minutes.

Remove the pan from the heat and gradually stir in the flour mixture. Return to the heat, bring to the boil and simmer for a further 5 minutes.

Ladle into warm, dry jars. Disperse any air pockets with a skewer or small knife and cover with screw-top lids. Label and leave to mature in a cool, dark place for at least 3 weeks.

To serve, partner with slivers of Parma ham.

Beetroot & Horseradish Relish

MAKES 3 jars
PREPARATION TIME 15 minutes
COOKING TIME about 1½ hours

500 g (1 lb) cooking apples, peeled, cored and halved
500 g (1 lb) raw beetroot, peeled
375 g (12 oz) onions, finely chopped
1 tablespoon finely chopped root ginger
5 cm (2 inch) raw horseradish root, peeled and grated
2 large garlic cloves, crushed
1 teaspoon paprika
250 g (8 oz) soft dark brown sugar
450 ml (¾ pint) red wine vinegar

Grate the apples and beetroot into a large saucepan, then add all the remaining ingredients.

Bring to the boil, then reduce the heat and simmer, covered, stirring occasionally, for about 1½ hours, until the relish has thickened and the beetroot is tender.

Ladle into warm, dry jars. Disperse any air pockets with a skewer or small knife and cover with screw-top lids. Label and leave to mature in a cool, dark place for about 1 week.

To serve, partner this relish with pork chops.

Carrot & Coriander Chutney

MAKES 4 jars
PREPARATION TIME 25 minutes
COOKING TIME 1–1¼ hours

1 kg (2 lb) carrots, coarsely grated
1 onion, chopped
1 large cooking apple, peeled, cored and diced
4 cm (1½ inch) piece root ginger, peeled and finely chopped
4 garlic cloves, finely chopped
125 g (4 oz) sultanas

1 litre (1¾ pints) distilled malt vinegar
250 g (8 oz) granulated sugar
2 teaspoons curry powder
2 teaspoons black mustard seeds (optional)
½ teaspoon salt
a little pepper
small bunch of coriander, roughly chopped

Add all the ingredients, except the coriander, to a preserving pan. Bring to the boil, then leave to simmer, uncovered, for 1–1¼ hours, stirring from time to time, until the chutney is thick.

Remove from the heat and stir in the coriander.

Ladle into warm, dry jars, filling to the very top and pressing down well. Disperse any air pockets with a skewer or small knife and cover with screw-top lids. Label and leave to mature in a cool, dark place for at least 3 weeks.

Aubergine &
Chilli Chutney

MAKES 4 jars
PREPARATION TIME 30 minutes
COOKING TIME 1½–1¾ hours

1 kg (2 lb) or 4 medium aubergines, diced

300 g (10 oz) or 3 red onions, chopped

500 g (1 lb) tomatoes, skinned (optional) and roughly chopped

4 cloves garlic, finely chopped

1–2 large mild red chillies, deseeded and finely chopped

200 g (7 oz) stoned dates, diced

300 ml (½ pint) red wine vinegar

250 g (8 oz) light muscovado sugar

2 teaspoons coriander seeds, roughly crushed

2 teaspoons cumin seeds, roughly crushed

1 teaspoon paprika

1 teaspoon salt

4 tablespoons chopped coriander

Add all the ingredients, except the mint, to a preserving pan. Cover and cook over a gentle heat for 1 hour, stirring from time to time, until softened. Remove the lid and cook for 30–45 minutes until thick, stirring more frequently towards the end of cooking as the chutney thickens.

Remove from the heat and stir in the coriander.

Ladle into warm, dry jars, filling to the very top and pressing down well. Disperse any air pockets with a skewer or small knife and cover with screw-top lids. Label and leave to mature in a cool, dark place for at least 3 weeks.

To serve, this chutney is delicious as a mezze starter with olives, marinated peppers, yogurt mixed with chopped mint, and griddled pitta bread.

Chestnut, Onion & Fennel Chutney

MAKES 1 jar
PREPARATION TIME 15 minutes
COOKING TIME 1 hour 25 minutes–1 hour 30 minutes

60 ml (2½ fl oz) olive oil
4 large red onions,
    thinly sliced
1 fennel bulb, trimmed and
    thinly sliced
250 g (8 oz) chestnuts,
    cooked, peeled and halved

100 g (3½ oz) soft light
    brown sugar
125 ml (4 fl oz) cider vinegar
125 ml (4 fl oz) sweet sherry
    or marsala wine
a little pepper

Heat the oil in a large saucepan, add the onions and fennel and cook over a gentle heat for 25–30 minutes until the onions are very soft.

Add the chestnuts, sugar, vinegar and sherry to the pan, season well with pepper and stir. Simmer gently, uncovered, for about 1 hour, stirring from time to time, until the chutney has thickened.

Ladle into warm, dry jars. Disperse any air pockets with a skewer or small knife and cover with screw-top lids. Label and leave to mature in a cool, dark place for at least 3 weeks.

To serve, this chutney goes well with rustic bread topped with blue cheese.

Coriander &
Gingered Parsnip Chutney

MAKES 4 jars
PREPARATION TIME 25 minutes
COOKING TIME 1–1¼ hours

1 kg (2 lb) parsnips, peeled
   and grated
1 onion, chopped
1 large cooking apple, peeled,
   cored, quartered and diced
4 cm (1½ inch) piece root
   ginger, peeled and finely
   chopped
4 garlic cloves, finely chopped
125 g (4 oz) sultanas

1 litre (1¾ pints) distilled
   malt vinegar
250 g (8 oz) granulated sugar
2 teaspoons curry powder
1 teaspoon dried red chillies,
   crushed
½ teaspoon salt
a little pepper
small bunch of coriander,
   roughly chopped

Add all the ingredients, except the coriander, to a preserving pan. Bring to the boil, then leave to simmer, uncovered, for 1–1¼ hours, stirring from time to time, until the chutney is thick.

Remove from the heat and stir in the coriander.

Ladle into warm, dry jars, filling to the very top and pressing down well. Disperse any air pockets with a skewer or small knife and cover with screw-top lids. Label and leave to mature in a cool, dark place for at least 3 weeks.

Hot Chilli & Tamarind Chutney

MAKES 2 jars
PREPARATION TIME 15 minutes
COOKING TIME 30 minutes

500 g (1 lb) red or green finger chillies
6 garlic cloves, crushed
2 tablespoons ground cumin
2 tablespoons ground turmeric
1 tablespoon tamarind paste
1 large onion, finely chopped
1 tablespoon salt
25 g (1 oz) root ginger, peeled and grated
300 ml (½ pint) groundnut oil
3 tablespoons muscovado sugar
300 ml (½ pint) white wine vinegar
grated rind and juice of 1 lime

Remove the stalks from the chillies, then finely chop the chillies, seeds and all.

Add the chillies, garlic, cumin, turmeric, tamarind, onion, salt, ginger and oil to a large saucepan and fry for 15 minutes, stirring frequently. Add the sugar, vinegar, the lime juice and rind and bring to the boil. Reduce the heat to medium and simmer, covered, for 10 minutes, stirring from time to time.

Ladle into warm, dry jars. Disperse any air pockets with a skewer or small knife and cover with screw-top lids. Label and leave to mature in a cool, dark place for at least 3 weeks. Stir the chutney well before using as the oil will separate out on standing.

To serve, partner this chutney with curry.

Green Tomato & Mango Chutney

MAKES 4 jars
PREPARATION TIME 15 minutes
COOKING TIME 1¼–1½ hours

1 kg (2 lb) green tomatoes, finely chopped
500 g (1 lb) onions, finely chopped
1 large, ripe mango, peeled, stoned and diced
2 fresh green chillies, halved, deseeded and finely chopped
2 garlic cloves, crushed

1 teaspoon ground ginger
pinch of ground cloves
pinch of ground turmeric
50 g (2 oz) raisins
100 g (3½ oz) dried apricots, chopped
250 g (8 oz) soft dark brown sugar
300 ml (½ pint) white wine vinegar

Add the tomatoes, onions, mango and chillies to a large pan and mix together. Add the garlic, ginger, cloves and turmeric, then stir in the raisins, apricot, sugar and vinegar.

Bring to the boil, then reduce the heat and simmer, covered, for 1¼–1½ hours, or until the chutney has thickened, stirring frequently.

Ladle into warm, dry jars. Disperse any air pockets with a skewer or small knife and cover with screw-top lids. Label and leave to mature in a cool, dark place for at least 3 weeks.

Sweet Potato, Ginger & Orange Chutney

MAKES 5 jars
PREPARATION TIME 30 minutes
COOKING TIME 1¾–2 hours

750 g (1½ lb) sweet potatoes,
peeled and diced
500 g (1 lb) onions, chopped
250 g (8 oz) sultanas
250 g (8 oz) carrots, coarsely
grated
2 oranges, finely chopped,
including pith and peel
4 garlic cloves, finely chopped
5 cm (2 inch) piece root ginger,
peeled and finely chopped

300 g (10 oz) light muscovado
sugar
750 ml (1¼ pints) distilled
malt vinegar
1½ teaspoons dried crushed
chillies
1 teaspoon salt
1 teaspoon black pepper,
roughly crushed

Add all the ingredients to a preserving pan, cover and cook gently for 1 hour, stirring occasionally. Remove the lid and cook for ¾–1 hour, stirring more frequently towards the end of cooking as the chutney thickens.

Ladle into warm, dry jars, filling to the very top and pressing down well. Disperse any air pockets with a skewer or small knife and cover with screw-top lids. Label and leave to mature in a cool, dark place for at least 3 weeks.

Sweet Potato & Orange Chutney

MAKES 5 jars
PREPARATION TIME 30 minutes
COOKING TIME 1¾–2 hours

750 g (1½ lb) sweet potatoes, peeled and diced
500 g (1 lb) onions, chopped
250 g (8 oz) sultanas
250 g (8 oz) carrots, coarsely grated
2 oranges, finely chopped, including pith and peel
4 garlic cloves, finely chopped
45 g tamarind pulp

300 g (10 oz) light muscovado sugar
750 ml (1¼ pints) distilled malt vinegar
1½ teaspoons dried crushed chillies
1 teaspoon salt
1 teaspoon black peppercorns, roughly crushed

Add all the ingredients to a preserving pan, cover and cook gently for 1 hour, stirring from time to time.

Remove the lid and cook for a further ¾–1 hour, stirring more frequently towards the end of cooking as the chutney thickens.

Ladle into warm, dry jars, filling to the very top and pressing down well. Disperse any air pockets with a skewer or small knife and cover with screw-top lids.

Label and leave to mature in a cool, dark place for at least 3 weeks.

To serve, this chutney will enhance any cheese or charcuterie board.

Chillied Tomato Jelly

MAKES 4 jars
PREPARATION TIME 30 minutes + straining
COOKING TIME 1 hour 20 minutes–1 hour 30 minutes

250 g (8 oz) red onions, roughly chopped

125 g (4 oz) celery, roughly chopped

1 kg (2 lb) tomatoes, roughly chopped (not skinned or deseeded)

500 g (1 lb) cooking apples, any bruised areas cut away, roughly chopped (not peeled or cored)

600 ml (1 pint) water

200 ml (7 fl oz) red wine vinegar

about 1.25 kg (2½ lb) granulated sugar

1 tablespoon tomato purée

1 teaspoon dried red chillies, crushed

juice of 2 lemons

15 g (½ oz) butter (optional)

50 g (2 oz) sun-blush tomatoes in oil, drained and diced

4 tablespoons vodka (optional)

Add the onions, celery, tomatoes and apples to a preserving pan. Pour in the measurement water and vinegar, then bring to the boil. Reduce the heat, cover and simmer gently for 1 hour, stirring and mashing from time to time with a fork, until the tomatoes and apples are pulpy.

Allow to cool slightly, pour into a scalded jelly bag suspended over a large bowl and allow to drip for several hours.

Measure the clear liquid and then pour back into the rinsed preserving pan. Weigh 500 g (1 lb) sugar for every 600 ml (1 pint) of liquid, then pour into the preserving pan. Add the tomato purée, chillies and lemon juice and heat gently, stirring from time to time, until the sugar has dissolved.

Bring to the boil, then boil rapidly until setting point is reached (20–30 minutes).

Skim with a draining spoon or stir in the butter, if needed. Stir in the sun-blush tomatoes and vodka, if liked, and leave to stand for 15 minutes so that the tomatoes don't rise in the jelly when potted. Ladle into warm, dry jars, filling to the very top. Cover with screw-top lids, or with waxed discs and cellophane tops secured with elastic bands. Label and leave to cool.

To serve, this jelly goes well with cold meats, such as salami and Parma ham, olives and sun-blush tomatoes.

Veg-Forward

Green Tomato Chutney

MAKES 4 jars
PREPARATION TIME 15 minutes
COOKING TIME 1¼–1½ hours

1 kg (2 lb) green tomatoes, finely chopped
500 g (1 lb) onions, finely chopped
500 g (1 lb) cooking apples, peeled, cored and chopped
2 fresh green chillies, halved, deseeded and finely chopped
2 garlic cloves, crushed

1 teaspoon ground ginger
generous pinch of ground cloves
generous pinch of ground turmeric
50 g (2 oz) raisins
250 g (8 oz) soft dark brown sugar
300 ml (½ pint) white wine vinegar

Add the tomatoes, onions, apples and chillies to a large pan and mix together. Add the garlic, ginger, cloves and turmeric, then stir in the raisins, sugar and vinegar.

Bring to the boil, then reduce the heat and simmer, covered, for 1¼–1½ hours, or until the chutney has thickened, stirring frequently.

Ladle into warm, dry jars. Disperse any air pockets with a skewer or small knife and cover with screw-top lids. Label and leave to mature in a cool, dark place for at least 3 weeks.

Courgette &
Mixed Bean Chutney

MAKES 6 jars
PREPARATION TIME 25 minutes
COOKING TIME about 35 minutes

750 g (1½ lb) mixed green, black and yellow French beans, trimmed
250 g (8 oz) runner beans, trimmed
900 ml (1½ pints) distilled malt vinegar
750 g (1½ lb) demerara sugar
500 g (1 lb) onions, chopped

250 g (8 oz) courgettes, diced
1½ tablespoons turmeric
1½ tablespoons mustard powder
3 tablespoons black mustard seeds
3 tablespoons cornflour
1 teaspoon salt
a little pepper
3 tablespoons water

Half-fill a preserving pan with water, bring to the boil, then add the beans. Return to the boil and cook for 2–3 minutes. Drain into a colander, refresh with cold water, then drain again. Thinly slice the cooled beans or roughly chop in a food processor.

Add the vinegar and sugar to the drained preserving pan, then add the onions and courgettes. Cover and bring to the boil, then reduce the heat and simmer for 10 minutes.

Mix the remaining dry ingredients together in a bowl, then stir in the measurement water until smooth. Stir this into the vinegar mixture, then simmer, uncovered, for 10 minutes, stirring until smooth and thickened.

Stir the blanched beans into the vinegar mixture and cook gently for 10 minutes, stirring frequently until just tender. Ladle into warm, dry jars, pressing the beans down well in the vinegar mix. Disperse any air pockets with a skewer or small knife and cover with screw-top lids. Label and leave to mature in a cool, dark place for at least 3 weeks.

Sweet Pickled Cucumbers

MAKES 3 jars
PREPARATION TIME 25 minutes + soaking
COOKING TIME 5–6 minutes

2 large cucumbers, thinly
  sliced
1 medium onion, thinly sliced
50 g (2 oz) salt
450 ml (¾ pint) white wine
  vinegar
375 g (12 oz) granulated sugar

½ teaspoon turmeric
2 teaspoons fennel seeds
½ teaspoon dried crushed
  red chillies
¼ teaspoon peppercorns,
  roughly crushed

Layer the cucumbers, onion and salt in a bowl, cover with a plate and weight down, then set aside for 4 hours.

Meanwhile, pour the vinegar into a saucepan, add the sugar and the remaining ingredients and heat gently, stirring from time to time, until the sugar has dissolved, then leave to cool.

Tip the cucumber and onion into a colander and drain off the liquid. Rinse with plenty of cold water and drain well.

Reheat the vinegar mixture until just boiling, add the drained cucumber and onion, cook for 1 minute, then lift out of the vinegar with a draining spoon and pack into warm, dry jars. Boil the remaining vinegar mixture for 4–5 minutes until syrupy, then leave to cool.

Pour the cold vinegar mixture over the cucumber slices to completely cover and fill the jars to the top (adding a little extra vinegar if needed). Screw on lids, label and leave to mature in a cool, dark place for 3–4 weeks.

Pickled Shallots

MAKES 1 very large jar
PREPARATION TIME 30 minutes +
soaking & standing
COOKING TIME 5 minutes

625 g (1¼ lb) small shallots
40 g (1½ oz) salt
450 ml (¾ pint) sherry vinegar
125 g (4 oz) caster sugar
125 g (4 oz) light muscovado
  sugar
2 garlic cloves, unpeeled

4 small bay leaves
4 sprigs thyme
4 sprigs rosemary
pinch of salt
½ teaspoon peppercorns,
  roughly crushed

Trim a little off the tops and roots of the shallots, then put into a bowl and cover with boiling water. Leave to soak for 3 minutes, then pour off the water and re-cover with cold water. Lift the shallots out one at a time and peel off the brown skins. Drain and layer in a bowl with the salt. Leave overnight.

Tip the shallots into a colander and drain off as much liquid as possible. Rinse with cold water, drain and dry with kitchen paper.

Add the vinegar and sugar to a saucepan with the garlic cloves, half the herbs, the salt and peppercorns. Heat gently until the sugar dissolves, stirring from time to time. Increase the heat to medium and simmer for 5 minutes. Leave to cool.

Pack the shallots tightly into a warm, dry jar with the remaining herbs. Strain and pour the cold vinegar syrup over the shallots, making sure that the shallots are covered with the vinegar to the very top. Then, cover with a screw-top lid. Label and leave to mature in a cool, dark place for 3–4 weeks.

Chilli Spiced Beetroot

MAKES 3 jars
PREPARATION TIME 25 minutes
COOKING TIME 33–63 minutes

1 kg (2 lb) or about 10 beetroot, leaves trimmed to about 2 cm (¾ inch) from the tops
600 ml (1 pint) malt vinegar
125 g (4 oz) granulated sugar
1 teaspoon dried red chilli flakes, crushed

3 star anise
4 teaspoons allspice berries, roughly crushed
½ teaspoon black peppercorns, roughly crushed
½ teaspoon salt

Cook the beetroot in a saucepan of boiling water for 30–60 minutes, depending on their size, or until a knife can be inserted into the largest one easily. Drain, leave to cool, then peel off the skins with a small knife.

Meanwhile, pour the vinegar into a saucepan, add the sugar and remaining ingredients. Heat gently, stirring from time to time, until the sugar has dissolved. Increase the heat and simmer for 3 minutes, then remove from the heat and leave to cool.

Cut the beetroot into chunks and pack into warm, dry jars. Pour over the cold vinegar mixture to cover the beetroot completely and so that the vinegar comes to the top of the jars (adding a little extra vinegar if needed). Screw on lids, label and leave to mature in a cool, dark place for 3–4 weeks.

To serve, try tossing some mixed lettuce leaves in a crème fraîche dressing, then top with flakes of peppered smoked mackerel and spoonfuls of drained beetroot with just a little of the vinegar mixture.

Chillied Pickled Shallots

MAKES 1 very large jar
PREPARATION TIME 30 minutes +
soaking & standing
COOKING TIME 5 minutes

625 g (1¼ lb) small shallots
40 g (1½ oz) salt
450 ml (¾ pint) sherry vinegar
125 g (4 oz) caster sugar
125 g (4 oz) light muscovado
sugar
2 garlic cloves, unpeeled

4 small bay leaves
1½ teaspoons dried chillies,
crushed
pinch of salt
½ teaspoon peppercorns,
roughly crushed

Trim a little off the tops and roots of the shallots, then put into a bowl and cover with boiling water. Leave to soak for 3 minutes, then pour off the water and re-cover with cold water. Lift the shallots out one at a time and peel off the brown skins. Drain and layer in a bowl with the salt. Leave overnight.

Tip the shallots into a colander and drain off as much liquid as possible. Rinse with cold water, drain and dry with kitchen paper.

Add the vinegar and sugar to a saucepan with the garlic cloves, half the herbs, the salt and peppercorns. Heat gently until the sugar dissolves, stirring from time to time. Increase the heat to medium and simmer for 5 minutes. Leave to cool.

Pack the shallots tightly into a warm, dry jar with the remaining herbs. Strain and pour the cold vinegar syrup over the shallots, making sure that the shallots are covered with the vinegar to the very top. Cover with a screw-top lid. Label and leave to mature in a cool, dark place for 3–4 weeks.

Chilli & Garlic Chutney

MAKES 2 jars
PREPARATION TIME 15 minutes
COOKING TIME 30 minutes

500 g (1 lb) red or green
   finger chillies
6 garlic cloves, crushed
4 tablespoons ground cumin
2 tablespoons ground
   turmeric
1 large onion, finely chopped

1 tablespoon salt
25 g (1 oz) root ginger, grated
300 ml (½ pint) groundnut oil
3 tablespoons muscovado
   sugar
300 ml (½ pint) white wine
   vinegar

Remove the stalks from the chillies, then finely chop the chillies, seeds and all.

Add the chillies, garlic, cumin, turmeric, onion, salt, ginger and oil to a large saucepan and fry for 15 minutes, stirring frequently. Add the sugar and vinegar and bring to the boil. Reduce the heat to medium and simmer, covered, for 10 minutes, stirring from time to time.

Ladle into warm, dry jars. Disperse any air pockets with a skewer or small knife and cover with screw-top lids. Label and leave to mature in a cool, dark place for at least 3 weeks. Stir the chutney well before using as the oil will separate out on standing.

To serve, partner this with curry.

Pickled Garlic

MAKES 2 small jars
PREPARATION TIME 15 minutes + standing
COOKING TIME 3–4 minutes

4 garlic bulbs
50 g (2 oz) salt
250 ml (8 fl oz) rice vinegar
100 g (3½ oz) granulated sugar

2 Thai green or red chillies,
  sliced
10 white peppercorns

Separate garlic bulbs into cloves, then peel and cut each clove in half.

Layer the garlic and salt in a bowl, cover with a plate, weigh down and leave to stand overnight.

Tip the garlic into a colander and drain off as much liquid as possible. Rinse with cold water, drain and dry with kitchen paper.

Add the vinegar, sugar, chillies and peppercorns to a saucepan, heat gently until the sugar has dissolved, then bring to the boil and cook over a medium heat for 2–3 minutes. Add the garlic and cook for 1 minute.

Pack the garlic and hot syrup into warm, dry jars, pressing the garlic below the vinegar mixture so that it is completely covered and the jar filled to the very top. Cover with screw-top lids. Label and leave to mature in a cool, dark place for 3–4 weeks.

Pickled Baby Peppers

MAKES 2 jars
PREPARATION TIME 15 minutes
COOKING TIME 7–8 minutes

500 g (1 lb) mixed baby red,
  yellow and orange peppers
450 ml (¾ pint) cider vinegar
  or white wine vinegar
4 tablespoons set honey
4 tablespoons light
  muscovado sugar
4 bay leaves

4 sprigs thyme
4 garlic cloves, sliced
2.5 cm (1 inch) piece root
  ginger, peeled and finely
  chopped
1 teaspoon coriander seeds
1 teaspoon salt

Add the peppers to a saucepan of boiling water and cook
for 2–3 minutes until just softened. Tip into a colander,
rinse with cold water and drain well.

Pour the vinegar into the drained pan and add all the
remaining ingredients. Heat gently until the sugar has
dissolved, then cook over a medium heat for 5 minutes.

Pack the peppers and herbs tightly into jars, then pour
over the hot vinegar mixture, making sure that the peppers
are completely covered by the vinegar. Cover with screw-top
lids. Label and leave to mature in a cool, dark place for
3–4 weeks.

Pickled Red Peppers

MAKES 1 jar
PREPARATION TIME 5 minutes
COOKING TIME 13 minutes

4 red peppers
600 ml (1 pint) distilled
   malt vinegar

250 g (8 oz) granulated sugar

Cut the tops off the red peppers and scoop out the core and seeds. Add to a saucepan of boiling water and cook for 3 minutes until just softened. Drain well, then dry on kitchen paper.

Heat the vinegar with the sugar until the sugar has dissolved, then cover and simmer for 10 minutes.

Pack the peppers tightly into a warm, dry jar. Pour the hot vinegar, making sure that the peppers are completely covered, and screw on the lid. Label and leave to mature in a cool, dark place for 3–4 weeks.

Pickled Red Cabbage

MAKES 3 jars
PREPARATION TIME 30 minutes +
soaking & standing
COOKING TIME 2 minutes

1 medium red cabbage,
  finely shredded
200 g (7 oz) courgettes, sliced
1 fennel bulb, sliced
100 g (3½ oz) salt
1.14 litre bottle distilled malt
  vinegar or white wine
  vinegar
250 g (8 oz) granulated sugar
2 teaspoons caraway seeds

2 teaspoons coriander seeds,
  roughly crushed
½ teaspoon peppercorns,
  roughly crushed
small dried red chillies,
  to taste
6 garlic cloves, halved
4 sprigs dill or fennel

Layer the vegetables in a bowl with the salt, cover with a plate and weigh down, then leave to soak overnight.

Pour the vinegar into a saucepan and add the sugar, caraway seeds, coriander seeds and peppercorns, then the dried chillies, garlic and 3 sprigs of dill or fennel.

Bring to the boil, stirring until the sugar has dissolved, then set aside for the flavours to mingle.

Next day, drain off the liquid from the vegetables. Pack into warm, dry jars with the halved garlic and chillies and the remaining sprigs of dill or fennel. Discard the cooked herbs from the spiced vinegar, then pour the cold vinegar mixture into the jars to the very top of the jars, making sure that the vegetables are completely covered (there is no need to strain the vinegar first).

Screw on the lids, label and leave to mature in a cool, dark place for 3–4 weeks.

Spiced Pickled Beetroot

MAKES 3 jars
PREPARATION TIME 25 minutes
COOKING TIME 33–63 minutes

1 kg (2 lb) or about 10
   beetroot, leaves trimmed
   to about 2 cm (¾ inch) from
   the tops
600 ml (1 pint) malt vinegar
125 g (4 oz) granulated sugar
3.5 cm (1½ inch) piece root
   ginger, peeled and finely
   chopped

4 teaspoons allspice berries,
   roughly crushed
½ teaspoon black
   peppercorns, roughly
   crushed
½ teaspoon salt

Cook the beetroot in a saucepan of boiling water for 30–60 minutes, depending on their size, or until a knife can be inserted into the largest one easily. Drain, leave to cool, then peel off the skins with a small knife.

Meanwhile, pour the vinegar into a saucepan and add the remaining ingredients. Heat gently, stirring from time to time, until the sugar has dissolved. Increase the heat and simmer for 3 minutes, then remove from the heat and leave to cool.

Cut the beetroot into chunks and pack into warm, dry jars. Pour over the cold vinegar mixture to cover the beetroot completely and so that the vinegar comes to the top of the jars (adding a little extra vinegar if needed). Screw on lids, label and leave to mature in a cool, dark place for 3–4 weeks.

To serve, try tossing some mixed lettuce leaves in a crème fraîche dressing, then top with flakes of peppered smoked mackerel and spoonfuls of drained beetroot with just a little of the vinegar mixture.

Curried Bean Pickle

MAKES 4 jars
PREPARATION TIME 25 minutes
COOKING TIME 23 minutes

250 g (8 oz) podded broad beans
250 g (8 oz) French beans, each cut into three
250 g (8 oz) runner beans, thinly sliced
500 ml (17 fl oz) distilled malt vinegar
375 g (12 oz) caster sugar
2 medium onions, chopped

3 garlic cloves, finely chopped
2 tablespoons cornflour
1 tablespoon turmeric
2 tablespoons mild curry powder
2 teaspoons fennel seeds, roughly crushed
1 teaspoon salt
a little pepper
2 tablespoons water

Bring a large saucepan of water to the boil, add the beans, cover and bring back to the boil, then cook for 3 minutes. Drain and refresh with cold water, then drain again.

Pour the vinegar and sugar into a preserving pan, add the onions and garlic, then cover and bring to the boil. Reduce the heat and simmer for 10 minutes.

Mix the remaining dry ingredients together in a bowl, then mix to a smooth paste with the measurement water. Stir into the vinegar mixture and cook, uncovered, for 5 minutes, stirring until thickened slightly.

Add the blanched vegetables, cook for a further 5 minutes, stirring, until the vegetables are just tender, then ladle into warm, dry jars, pressing the vegetables down below the liquid with a fork and making sure there are no air pockets. Label and leave to mature in a cool, dark place for 3–4 weeks.

Hot Sweetcorn Relish

MAKES 3 jars
PREPARATION TIME 15 minutes
COOKING TIME 25 minutes

4 tablespoons corn oil
2 large onions, finely chopped
1 green pepper, cored, deseeded and finely chopped
1 red pepper, cored, deseeded and finely chopped
4 celery sticks, finely chopped
1 teaspoon salt
1 large garlic clove, crushed

2 carrots, peeled and cut into small cubes
50 g (2 oz) sugar
2 teaspoons mustard powder
1 teaspoon smoked paprika
1 teaspoon dried red chillies, crushed
750 g (1½ lb) frozen sweetcorn
450 ml (¾ pint) cider vinegar

Heat the oil in a large saucepan and add the onions, peppers and celery. Fry gently for 10 minutes until soft but not browned, then add the salt and garlic.

Add all the remaining ingredients and bring to the boil. Reduce the heat and cook, uncovered, for 15 minutes, stirring occasionally.

Ladle into warm, dry jars, pressing the vegetables well down into the juices, then top with screw-top lids and leave to cool.

This relish does not need time to mature but, if not immediately consumed, label unopened jars and store in a cool, dark place.

To serve, this relish makes a great accompaniment to homemade burgers.

Sweetcorn Relish

MAKES 3 jars
PREPARATION TIME 15 minutes
COOKING TIME 25 minutes

4 tablespoons corn oil
2 large onions, finely chopped
1 green pepper, cored, deseeded and finely chopped
1 red pepper, cored, deseeded and finely chopped
4 celery sticks, finely chopped
1 teaspoon salt
1 large garlic clove, crushed
2 carrots, peeled and cut into small cubes
50 g (2 oz) sugar
2 teaspoons mustard powder
750 g (1½ lb) frozen sweetcorn
450 ml (¾ pint) cider vinegar

Heat the oil in a large saucepan and add the onions, peppers and celery. Fry gently for 10 minutes until soft but not browned, then add the salt and garlic.

Add all the remaining ingredients and bring to the boil. Reduce the heat and cook, uncovered, for 15 minutes, stirring occasionally.

Ladle into warm, dry jars, pressing the vegetables well down into the juices, then top with screw-top lids and leave to cool. This relish does not need time to mature but, if not immediately consumed, label unopened jars and store in a cool, dark place.

Honey Pickled Chillies

MAKES 2 jars
PREPARATION TIME 15 minutes
COOKING TIME 7–8 minutes

500 g (1 lb) whole red finger chillies
450 ml (¾ pint) cider vinegar or white wine vinegar
4 tablespoons set honey
4 tablespoons light muscovado sugar
4 bay leaves
4 sprigs thyme
4 garlic cloves, sliced
2.5 cm (1 inch) piece root ginger, peeled and finely chopped
1 teaspoon coriander seeds
1 teaspoon salt

Add the chillies to a saucepan of boiling water and cook for 2–3 minutes until just softened. Tip into a colander, rinse with cold water and drain well.

Pour the vinegar into the drained pan and add all the remaining ingredients. Heat gently until the sugar has dissolved, then cook over a medium heat for 5 minutes.

Pack the chillies and herbs from the vinegar tightly into jars, then pour over the hot vinegar mixture, making sure that the chillies are completely covered by the vinegar. Cover with screw-top lids, label and leave to mature in a cool, dark place for 3–4 weeks.

Torshi

MAKES 3 jars
PREPARATION TIME 30 minutes +
soaking & standing
COOKING TIME 2 minutes

200 g (7 oz) courgettes, sliced
200 g (7 oz) carrots, sliced
150 g (5 oz) French beans,
  halved
1 fennel bulb, sliced
1 cauliflower, cut into small
  florets
250 g (8 oz) small pickling
  onions, peeled
100 g (3½ oz) salt
1.14 litre bottle distilled
  malt vinegar or white
  wine vinegar

250 g (8 oz) granulated sugar
2 teaspoons caraway seeds
2 teaspoons coriander seeds,
  roughly crushed
½ teaspoon peppercorns,
  roughly crushed
small dried red chillies, to
  taste
6 garlic cloves, peeled and
  halved
4 sprigs dill or fennel

Layer the vegetables in a bowl with the salt, cover with a plate and weigh down, then leave to soak overnight.

Pour the vinegar into a saucepan and add the sugar, caraway seeds, coriander seeds and peppercorns, then the dried chillies, garlic and 3 sprigs of dill or fennel.

Bring to the boil, stirring until the sugar has dissolved, then set aside for the flavours to infuse.

Next day, drain off the liquid from the vegetables, rinse with cold water, drain well, then pat dry with kitchen paper. Pack into warm, dry jars with the garlic and chillies from the vinegar mixture and the remaining dill or fennel. Discard the cooked herbs from the spiced vinegar, then pour the cold vinegar mixture into the jars to the very top of the jars, making sure that the vegetables are completely covered (there is no need to strain the vinegar first).

Secure the lids, label and leave to mature in a cool, dark place for 3–4 weeks.

Matcha Pickles

MAKES 2 large jars
PREPARATION TIME 10 minutes
COOKING TIME 10 minutes

FOR THE PICKLED EGGS

6 eggs
250 ml (9 fl oz) cider vinegar
150 ml (5 fl oz) water
50 g (2 oz) coconut sugar
1 teaspoon sea salt
1 teaspoon fennel seeds
1 teaspoon mustards seeds
3 bay leaves
1 whole green chilli
1 tablespoon matcha powder

FOR THE PICKLED VEGETABLES

1 large carrot, cut into batons
1 large cucumber, halved lengthways, deseeded and cut into batons
½ medium cauliflower, cut into small florets
¼ onion, sliced
250 ml (9 fl oz) brown rice vinegar
150 ml (5 fl oz) water
50 g (2 oz) coconut sugar
1 teaspoon sea salt
1 teaspoon matcha powder

Make the pickled eggs. Bring a pan of water to the boil. Add the eggs and boil for 6 minutes, then run under cold water before peeling and placing in a sterilized jar. Meanwhile, put all the remaining egg ingredients into a saucepan, bring to the boil and simmer for a couple of minutes.

Allow the pickling liquor to cool a little, then pour over the eggs. Seal and when cool, transfer to the refrigerator, where they will keep for up to 4 weeks.

Make the pickled vegetables. Place the prepared vegetables in a separate sterilized jar. Make the pickling liquor as above and pour over.

Turmeric Pickles

MAKES 3 jars
PREPARATION TIME 10 minutes
COOKING TIME 10–15 minutes

200 g (7 oz) daikon radish, peeled
200 g (7 oz) carrots, peeled
200 g (7 oz) turnips, peeled
5 curry leaves per jar (fresh or dried)
1 red chilli per jar, deseeded and halved lengthways
2 strips of lemon rind per jar

FOR THE PICKLING LIQUOR
1.2 litres (2 pints) warm water
160 ml (5½ fl oz) rice wine vinegar
5 tablespoons coconut sugar or granulated sugar
2 tablespoons sea salt
½ teaspoon ground turmeric

Quarter the daikon radish lengthways so you have 4 long pieces, then cut each quarter into chunks.

The carrots can be cut in half lengthways, then cut into chunky half-moons. You can cut the turnips any which way, as long as they are roughly the same size as the rest of the vegetables.

Divide them evenly between the jars but don't over-pack them. Add the curry leaves, chillies and strips of lemon rind to the jars.

Make the pickling liquor. Heat the measured water and vinegar in a saucepan over a very low heat until it is nearly hot, then dissolve the sugar, salt and turmeric in it.

Pour the liquor evenly between the jars so the vegetables are covered. You may need to press the veg down slightly. Seal the jars and put in the refrigerator for 3 days to pickle. If you don't have 3 days to spare, you can bring the liquor to the boil before pouring it onto the veg, sealing the jar and allowing it to cool down. You don't get quite the full flavour but you will still have decent pickled veg.

Enjoy with a slice of cheese, cold cuts or on picnics.

Fruit-Forward

Cranberry & Red Wine Chutney

MAKES 3 jars
PREPARATION TIME 30 minutes
COOKING TIME 1¼–1½ hours

500 g (1 lb) fresh or frozen cranberries
500 g (1 lb) red onions, thinly sliced
250 g (8 oz) mixed dried fruit
250 g (8 oz) light muscovado sugar
150 ml (¼ pint) red wine
150 ml (¼ pint) red wine vinegar
2 teaspoons ground mixed spice
1 teaspoon dried crushed chillies
1 teaspoon salt
½ teaspoon pepper

Add all the ingredients to a preserving pan, cover and simmer gently for 1 hour, stirring from time to time, until softened.

Remove the lid and cook for 15–30 minutes until thick, stirring more frequently towards the end of cooking, until the cranberries are very soft and the chutney is thick.

Spoon into warm, dry jars, filling to the very top and pressing down well. Disperse any air pockets with a skewer or small knife. Cover with screw-top lids, label and leave to cool.

Beetroot & Apple Relish

MAKES 3 jars
PREPARATION TIME 15 minutes
COOKING TIME about 1½ hours

500 g (1 lb) cooking apples, peeled, cored and halved
500 g (1 lb) raw beetroot, peeled
375 g (12 oz) onions, finely chopped
1 tablespoon finely chopped root ginger
2 large garlic cloves, crushed
1 teaspoon paprika
1 teaspoon ground turmeric
1 cinnamon stick
250 g (8 oz) soft dark brown sugar
450 ml (¾ pint) red wine vinegar

Grate the apples and beetroot into a large saucepan, then add all the remaining ingredients.

Bring to the boil, then reduce the heat and simmer, covered, stirring occasionally, for about 1½ hours, until the relish has thickened and the beetroot is tender.

Ladle into warm, dry jars. Disperse any air pockets with a skewer or small knife and cover with screw-top lids. Label and leave to mature in a cool, dark place for about 1 week.

To serve, partner this relish with pork chops.

Gooseberry Relish
with Cardamom

MAKES 2 jars
PREPARATION TIME 25 minutes
COOKING TIME 45 minutes

1 kg (2 lb) gooseberries, topped and tailed
2 onions, chopped
10 cardamom pods, crushed

300 ml (½ pint) distilled malt vinegar
250 g (8 oz) granulated sugar
1 teaspoon salt
a little pepper

Add all the ingredients to a preserving pan.

Cook gently, uncovered, for 45 minutes until the gooseberries are soft, stirring from time to time, but more frequently towards the end of cooking as the relish thickens.

Ladle into warm, dry jars, pressing down well and filling the jars to the tops. Disperse any air pockets with a skewer or small knife and cover with screw-top lids.

Label and leave to mature in a cool, dark place for at least 3 weeks.

To serve, this relish is very tasty with pork pie, little gem lettuce leaves and spring onions.

Pickled Lemons
with Chilli & Garlic

MAKES 1 large jar
PREPARATION TIME 10 minutes

8 unwaxed baby lemons
8 unpeeled garlic cloves
4 dried chillies
1 teaspoon coriander seeds

1 small cinnamon stick,
   bruised
2 bay leaves
50 g (2 oz) salt
juice of 1 lemon

Sprinkle a little salt into the bottom of a large, wide-necked jar, then layer the lemons, garlic, chillies, spices, bay leaves and remaining salt in the jar.

Add the lemon juice and enough boiling water to cover the lemons. Top with an airtight lid and leave in a warm place for at least 2 weeks before using, for the lemon skins to soften. A white film may appear on the jar or on the lemons – this is harmless and can be rinsed off.

Preserved Lemons

MAKES 1 large jar
PREPARATION TIME 10 minutes

8 unwaxed baby lemons
1 teaspoon coriander seeds
1 small cinnamon stick,
  bruised

2 bay leaves
50 g (2 oz) salt
juice of 1 lemon

Sprinkle a little salt into the bottom of a large, wide-necked jar, then layer the lemons, spices, bay leaves and remaining salt in the jar.

Add the lemon juice and enough boiling water to cover the lemons. Top with an airtight lid and leave in a warm place for at least 2 weeks before using, for the lemon skins to soften. A white film may appear on the jar or on the lemons – this is harmless and can be rinsed off.

Sweet Pickled Oranges

MAKES 3 jars
PREPARATION TIME 10 minutes
COOKING TIME 1 hour–1 hour 10 minutes

6 thin-skinned oranges,
  thinly sliced
450 ml (¾ pint) white wine
  vinegar
375 g (12 oz) granulated sugar
1 medium onion, thinly sliced

½ teaspoon turmeric
2 teaspoons fennel seeds
½ teaspoon dried crushed
  red chillies
¼ teaspoon peppercorns,
  roughly crushed

Put the oranges into a saucepan, cover with water and bring
to the boil. Simmer for 45 minutes until tender. Drain.

Pour the vinegar into a saucepan, add the sugar and the
remaining ingredients and heat gently, stirring from time to
time, until the sugar has dissolved. Add the cooked orange
slices and simmer for 10 minutes, or until the orange rind
becomes transparent.

Lift out the oranges with a slotted spoon and pack into
warm, dry jars. Boil the remaining vinegar mixture for
4–5 minutes until syrupy, then leave to cool.

Pour the cold vinegar mixture over the orange slices to
completely cover and to fill the jars to the top (adding a little
extra vinegar if needed). Screw on lids, label and leave to
mature in a cool, dark place for 3–4 weeks.

Pickled Kumquats

MAKES 1 large jar
PREPARATION TIME 10 minutes
COOKING TIME 5 minutes

30 kumquats, halved
125 g (4 oz) salt
1 tablespoon coriander seeds
2 teaspoons cumin seeds
1 teaspoon dried chilli seeds
1 tablespoon ground turmeric
1 teaspoon smoked paprika
300 ml (½ pint) vegetable oil

Put the kumquats into a large jar and cover with the salt.

Dry-fry the coriander and cumin seeds in a small nonstick frying pan, then coarsely grind them to a powder in a pestle and mortar, mix with the chilli seeds, turmeric and smoked paprika, then stir in the vegetable oil.

Pour the mixture over the kumquats and mix well.

Cover the jar with a clean cloth and leave to mature for 10 days in a bright, warm place. After this time, top with an airtight lid. Label and store in a cool, dark place.

Pickled Peaches

MAKES 1 large jar
PREPARATION TIME 25 minutes
COOKING TIME 6–8 minutes

300 ml (½ pint) white
 malt vinegar
500 g (1 lb) granulated sugar
1 teaspoon whole cloves
1 teaspoon whole allspice
 berries

1 cinnamon stick, halved
1 kg (2 lb) small peaches,
 halved and stoned

Pour the vinegar into a large saucepan, add the sugar and spices and heat gently until the sugar has dissolved.

Add the peach halves to the pan and cook very gently for 4–5 minutes until just tender but still firm. Lift out of the syrup with a slotted spoon and pack tightly into the jar.

Boil the syrup for 2–3 minutes to concentrate the flavours, then pour over the fruit, making sure that the fruit is completely covered and the jar filled to the very top. Top up with a little extra warm vinegar if needed. Add a small piece of crumpled greaseproof paper to stop the fruit from rising out of the vinegar in the jar. Screw or clip on the lid, label and leave to cool.

As the peaches become saturated with the syrup they will sink; at this point they will be ready to eat.

Andrew's Plums

MAKES 2 jars
PREPARATION TIME 25 minutes
COOKING TIME 1 hour

½ teaspoon cumin seeds
½ teaspoon fennel seeds
1 teaspoon coriander seeds
½ teaspoon dried chilli flakes
1 kg (2 lb) plums, halved,
  stoned and diced
1 onion, chopped

2.5 cm (1 inch) piece root
  ginger, peeled and finely
  chopped
150 ml (¼ pint) malt vinegar
125 g (4 oz) granulated sugar
2 tablespoons raisins
juice of 1 lemon
salt and pepper

Roughly crush the seeds in a pestle and mortar, then toast
in a hot preserving pan with the chilli flakes for a few
seconds. Add all the remaining ingredients, then cover and
simmer gently for 30 minutes, stirring occasionally.

Uncover the chutney and cook for 30 minutes, stirring
until thick and pulpy. Mash with a potato masher, or blitz in
a food processor, until smooth.

Ladle into warm, dry jars, filling to the very top and
pressing down well. Disperse any air pockets with a skewer
or small knife and cover with screw-top lids. Label and leave
to mature in a cool, dark place for at least 3 weeks.

To serve, add to a cheese and salad sandwich.

Herby Pickled Plums

MAKES 3 jars
PREPARATION TIME 20 minutes
COOKING TIME 3 minutes

750 ml (1¼ pints) white wine
    vinegar
500 g (1 lb) caster sugar
7 sprigs rosemary
7 sprigs thyme
7 small bay leaves
4 sprigs lavender (optional)

4 garlic cloves, unpeeled
1 teaspoon salt
½ teaspoon mixed
    peppercorns
1.5 kg (3 lb) firm red plums,
    washed and pricked

Pour the vinegar and sugar into a saucepan, add 4 each of
the rosemary and thyme sprigs and bay leaves, all the
lavender, if using, the garlic, salt and peppercorns. Cook
gently, stirring once or twice, until the sugar has dissolved.
Bring to the boil, then boil for 3 minutes until the mixture
becomes syrupy.

Pack the plums tightly into warm, dry jars and tuck the
remaining herbs into them. Strain in the hot vinegar,
making sure that the plums are completely covered, then
top with airtight lids.

Label and leave to mature in a cool, dark place for
3–4 weeks. The plums will lose colour slightly.

Plum & Star Anise Jelly

MAKES 7 jars
PREPARATION TIME 25 minutes + straining
COOKING TIME 40–50 minutes

2 kg (4 lb) whole plums
1.2 litres (2 pints) water
about 1.25 kg (2½ lb)
  granulated sugar

7 small star anise
15 g (½ oz) butter (optional)

Add the plums and measured water to a preserving pan.
Bring to the boil, then cover and cook gently for 30 minutes,
stirring and mashing the fruit from time to time with a fork,
until soft.

Cool slightly, then pour into a scalded jelly bag suspended
over a large bowl and allow to slowly drip.

Measure the clear liquid and pour back into the rinsed
preserving pan. Weigh 500 g (1 lb) sugar for every 600 ml
(1 pint) of liquid, then pour into the preserving pan. Add the
star anise and heat gently, stirring occasionally, until the
sugar has dissolved.

Bring to the boil, then boil rapidly until setting point is
reached (10–20 minutes). Skim with a draining spoon and
stir in the butter, if needed. Allow to stand for 5 minutes.

Ladle into warm, dry jars, filling to the very top, adding
1 star anise per jar. Cover with screw-top lids. Label and leave
to cool.

Plum & Crushed Peppercorn Jelly

MAKES 7 jars
PREPARATION TIME 25 minutes + straining
COOKING TIME 40–50 minutes

2 kg (4 lb) whole plums
1.2 litres (2 pints) water
about 1.25 kg (2½ lb)
  granulated sugar
2 teaspoons mixed
  peppercorns, roughly
  crushed

2 teaspoons pink
  peppercorns, either dried or
  in brine, roughly crushed
15 g (½ oz) butter (optional)

Add the plums and measured water to a preserving pan. Bring to the boil, then cover and cook gently for 30 minutes, stirring and mashing the fruit from time to time with a fork, until soft.

Allow to cool slightly, then pour into a scalded jelly bag suspended over a large bowl and allow to drip for several hours.

Measure the clear liquid and pour back into the rinsed preserving pan. Weigh 500 g (1 lb) sugar for every 600 ml (1 pint) of liquid, then pour into the preserving pan. Add the peppercorns and heat gently, stirring from time to time, until the sugar has dissolved.

Bring to the boil, then boil rapidly until setting point is reached (10–20 minutes). Skim with a draining spoon and stir in the butter if needed. Allow to stand for 5 minutes so that the peppercorns don't float to the surface.

Ladle into warm, dry jars, filling to the very top. Cover with screw-top lids, or with waxed discs and cellophane tops secured with elastic bands. Label and leave to cool.

To serve, this jelly works well with roast lamb and roast potatoes.

Gooseberry & Rosemary Jelly

MAKES 4 jars
PREPARATION TIME 25 minutes + straining
COOKING TIME 30–45 minutes

1.5 kg (3 lb) gooseberries (no need to top and tail)
1 litre (1¾ pints) water
4–5 sprigs rosemary

about 875 g (1¾ lb) granulated sugar
15 g (½ oz) butter (optional)

Add the gooseberries, measured water and rosemary to a preserving pan. Bring to the boil, then cover and simmer gently for 20–30 minutes, stirring and mashing the fruit from time to time with a fork, until soft.

Leave to cool slightly, then pour into a scalded jelly bag suspended over a large bowl and allow to drip for several hours.

Measure the clear liquid and pour back into the rinsed preserving pan. Weigh 500 g (1 lb) sugar for every 600 ml (1 pint) of liquid, then pour into the preserving pan. Heat gently, stirring from to time, until the sugar has dissolved.

Bring to the boil, then boil rapidly until setting point is reached (10–15 minutes). Skim with a draining spoon and stir in the butter if needed.

Ladle into warm, dry jars, filling to the very top. Cover with screw-top lids, or with waxed discs and cellophane tops secured with elastic bands. Label and leave to cool.

To serve, try this jelly with grilled herrings and salad.

Sour Apple & Rosemary Jelly

MAKES 4 jars
PREPARATION TIME 25 minutes + straining
COOKING TIME 30–45 minutes

1.5 kg (3 lb) cooking apples, roughly chopped (not peeled or cored)
750 ml (1¼ pints) water
150 ml (¼ pint) white wine

vinegar
4–5 sprigs rosemary
about 875 g (1¾ lb) granulated sugar
15 g (½ oz) butter (optional)

Add the apples, water, vinegar and rosemary to a preserving pan. Bring to the boil, then cover and simmer gently for 20–30 minutes, stirring and mashing the fruit from time to time with a fork, until soft.

Leave to cool slightly, then pour into a scalded jelly bag suspended over a large bowl and allow to drip for several hours.

Measure the clear liquid and pour back into the rinsed preserving pan. Weigh 500 g (1 lb) sugar for every 600 ml (1 pint) of liquid, then pour into the preserving pan. Heat gently, stirring from to time, until the sugar has dissolved.

Bring to the boil, then boil rapidly until setting point is reached (10–15 minutes). Skim with a draining spoon or stir in butter if needed.

Ladle into warm, dry jars, filling to the very top. Cover with screw-top lids, or with waxed discs and cellophane tops secured with elastic bands. Label and leave to cool.

To serve, try this jelly with grilled herrings and salad.

Pear & Red Wine Cheese

MAKES 2 jars
PREPARATION TIME 30 minutes
COOKING TIME 1¼–1½ hours

1.5 kg (3 lb) pears, peeled, cored, quartered and sliced
1 teaspoon cloves, roughly crushed
300 ml (½ pint) red wine

300 ml (½ pint) water
about 1.5 kg (3 lb) granulated sugar
15 g (½ oz) butter (optional)

Add the pears and cloves to a preserving pan. Pour over the wine and measurement water to just cover the base of the pan, then bring to the boil. Cover and cook gently for 30 minutes, stirring from time to time and breaking up the pears with a wooden spoon or fork, until very soft.

Allow to cool slightly, then purée in small batches in a food processor or blender, or press through a sieve.

Weigh the purée, then pour back into the rinsed preserving pan. Weigh 375 g (12 oz) sugar for every 500g (1lb) of purée. Heat gently, stirring from time to time, until the sugar has dissolved.

Cook over a medium heat for 45–60 minutes, stirring more frequently towards the end of cooking, until the mixture has darkened slightly and is so thick that the wooden spoon leaves a line across the base of the pan when drawn through the mixture. Skim with a draining spoon and stir in the butter if needed.

Ladle into warm, dry jars, filling to the very top. Clip on lids, label and leave to cool.

To serve, this makes a good accompaniment for cheese, crackers and grapes.

Plum & Clove Cheese

MAKES 2 jars
PREPARATION TIME 30 minutes
COOKING TIME 1¼–1½ hours

1.5 kg (3 lb) whole plums
1 teaspoon cloves, roughly
   crushed
300 ml (½ pint) red wine
600 ml (1 pint) water

about 1.5 kg (3 lb) granulated
   sugar
15 g (½ oz) butter (optional)

Count the plums, then add them and the cloves to a preserving pan. Pour over the wine and measurement water to the pan, then bring to the boil. Cover and cook gently for 30 minutes, stirring from time and breaking up the plums with a wooden spoon or potato masher, until very soft.

Allow to cool slightly. Remove the stones, making sure to count them to double-check that you have them all, then purée in small batches in a food processor or blender, or press through a sieve.

Weigh the purée, then pour back into the rinsed preserving pan. Weigh 375 g (12 oz) sugar for every 500g (1 lb) of purée. Heat gently, stirring from time to time, until the sugar has dissolved.

Cook over a medium heat for 45–60 minutes, stirring more frequently towards the end of cooking, until the mixture has darkened slightly and is so thick that the wooden spoon leaves a line across the base of the pan when drawn through the mixture. Skim with a draining spoon and stir in the butter if needed.

Ladle into warm, dry jars, filling to the very top. Clip on lids, label and leave to cool.

To serve, this makes a good accompaniment for cheese, crackers and grapes.

Sides, Sauces
& Dressings

G&T
Fridge Pickles

MAKES 1 jar
PREPARATION TIME 10 minutes

5–7 small pickling cucumbers (or a regular cucumber will do)
170ml (6fl oz) gin
170ml (6fl oz) tonic water

juice of 1 lime
2 tablespoons Rose's lime juice
1 tablespoon juniper berries

Wash the cucumbers and trim the tips. Slice them in half lengthways, and then in half again. Trim them to the length of your jar. You want the spears to fit into the jar and eventually be completely submerged in liquid .

Mix the gin, tonic water, fresh lime juice and the Rose's lime juice. Fit the spears into a clean, dry glass jar. Fill the jar but don't pack them in too tightly.

Lightly crush the juniper berries and add them to the jar along with the liquid mixture. Top off with more tonic water if the spears aren't completely submerged.

Cap the jar tightly and refrigerate. Let the cucumbers pickle for at least 2 days before eating. The pickles will keep for at least 6 weeks in the fridge.

Soured Cucumbers with Goats' Curd

SERVES 14
PREPARATION TIME 5 minutes
COOKING TIME 5 minutes + cooling & standing

FOR THE CUCUMBERS
200 ml (7 fl oz) white wine
  vinegar
2 tablespoons caster sugar
1 teaspoon pink peppercorns
1 tablespoon mustard seeds
2 baby cucumbers, cut into
  wedges
1 teaspoon sea salt
50 g (2 oz) dill

FOR THE MATCHA SALT
1 tablespoon sea salt flakes
½ teaspoon matcha powder

TO SERVE
120 g (4 oz) goats' curd
4 slices wholemeal bread,
  toasted
20 g (¾ oz) dill

Make the cucumbers. Heat the vinegar, sugar, peppercorns and mustard seeds in a saucepan, stirring until the sugar has dissolved. Set aside to cool.

Place the cucumber wedges in a colander and toss with the salt. Leave to stand for 15 minutes before transferring to a sterilized jar along with the dill. Pour over the cooled vinegar and seal with an airtight lid. The cucumbers will be sour enough to eat a day later, but will keep for up to 1 month in the refrigerator, becoming more sour over time.

Combine the salt and matcha powder in a small bowl.

To serve, spread the curd on a serving plate and arrange the cucumber wedges on top. Toast the bread and finish by sprinkling over the matcha salt, dill and a little pickling liquor.

Japanese Pickled Ginger

MAKES 2 small jars
PREPARATION TIME 15 minutes + standing
COOKING TIME 3–4 minutes

500 g (1 lb) root ginger, peeled
and very thinly sliced
50 g (2 oz) salt
250 ml (8 fl oz) rice vinegar

100 g (3½ oz) granulated sugar
2 Thai green or red chillies,
sliced
10 white peppercorns

Layer the ginger and salt in a bowl, cover with a plate, weigh
down and leave to stand overnight.

Tip the ginger into a colander and drain off as much liquid
as possible. Rinse with cold water, drain and dry with
kitchen paper.

Add the vinegar, sugar, chillies and peppercorns to
a saucepan, heat gently until the sugar has dissolved,
then bring to the boil and cook over a medium heat for
2–3 minutes. Add the ginger and cook for 1 minute.

Pack the ginger and hot syrup into warm, dry jars,
pressing the ginger below the vinegar mixture so that it is
completely covered and the jar filled to the very top. Cover
with screw-top lids. Label and leave to mature in a cool,
dark place for 3–4 weeks.

To serve, use as an accompaniment for sushi.

Chilli Jam

125 g (4 oz) mild red chillies, cored, deseeded and chopped
1 garlic clove, crushed
1 onion, chopped

5 cm (2 inch) piece root ginger, peeled and chopped
125 ml (4 fl oz) white vinegar
500 g (1 lb) granulated sugar

Place all the ingredients in a small saucepan and bring to the boil, then reduce the heat and simmer for 15 minutes. The mixture should be thick, sticky and jam-like, and will become more so as it cools.

Ladle into a warm, dry jar. Disperse any air pockets with a skewer or small knife and cover with a screw-top lid. Store in the refrigerator, for up to 1 week, and use it as an accompaniment to spice up griddled meats.

Pickled Peach Dressing

SERVES 2
PREPARATION TIME 5 minutes

2 tablespoons spiced syrup
    from the jar of peaches
    (see page 116)
3 tablespoons olive oil

2 tablespoons parsley or
    chives, finely chopped
100 g (3½ oz) washed salad
    leaves

Whisk the syrup with the olive oil and parsley or chives,
then toss with the salad leaves and serve immediately.

Spiced & Roasted Seeds

MAKES 1 small jar
PREPARATION TIME 5 minutes
COOKING TIME 30–40 minutes

100 g (3½ oz) pumpkin seeds
100 g (3½ oz) sunflower seeds
1 tablespoon olive oil
juice of 1 lime

juice of 1 orange
½ teaspoon ground turmeric
½ teaspoon mild chilli powder
½ teaspoon sea salt flakes

Preheat the oven to 180°C (350°F), Gas Mark 4. Line a baking tray with baking paper.

Mix all the ingredients together in a bowl, then spread out over the prepared tray. Roast for 30–40 minutes, shaking the seeds halfway through cooking, until golden and crunchy.

Allow to cool, then transfer to an airtight jar.

Turmeric-Infused Oil

MAKES 1 bottle
PREPARATION TIME 5 minutes

2 tablespoons grated fresh turmeric, or 2 heaped tablespoons ground turmeric

250 ml (8 fl oz) extra virgin olive oil
250 ml (8 fl oz) avocado oil
1 teaspoon coarsely ground black pepper

Add all the ingredients to a glass bottle, seal and shake. Leave to infuse for 2 weeks before using.

Turmeric Mustard

MAKES 1 small jar
PREPARATION TIME 5 minutes + standing

50 g (2 oz) mustard seeds
  (white or mixed)
25 g (1 oz) mustard powder
2 teaspoons sea salt flakes
150 ml (¼ fl oz) water

3 tablespoons apple cider
  vinegar
1 teaspoon ground turmeric
2 tablespoons raw clear
  (runny) honey

Mix the mustard seeds, mustard powder and salt in a bowl, then add the measured water, combining well. Set aside for 10 minutes before adding the vinegar, turmeric and honey. Mix well.

Transfer to an airtight jar and allow to set overnight in the refrigerator. The mustard will keep for up to 6 months in the refrigerator.

Recipes Index

Recipes are marked as being suitable for vegans (vg) or vegetarians (v)

UK/US Glossary

UK	US
aubergine	eggplant
baking tray	baking sheet
beetroot	beets
broad beans	fava beans
chilli	chili
chilli flakes	red pepper flakes
chips	fries
coriander	cilantro
cornflour	cornstarch
courgette	zucchini
flour (plain)	all-purpose
flour (wholemeal)	whole-wheat
frying pan	skillet
greaseproof paper	wax paper
grill	broil
jam	preserves
kitchen paper	paper towels
pepper (green/red/yellow)	bell pepper
prawn	shrimp
sieve	strainer
spring onion	scallion
stoned	pitted
sugar (caster)	superfine
sweetcorn	corn
tomato purée	tomato paste

Publisher's note:

Standard level spoon measurements are used in all recipes.
1 tablespoon = one 15 ml spoon
1 teaspoon = one 5 ml spoon

Both imperial and metric measurements have been given in all recipes. Use one set of measurements only and not a mixture of both.

Eggs should be medium unless otherwise stated. The Department of Health advises that eggs should not be consumed raw. This book contains dishes made with raw or lightly cooked eggs. It is prudent for more vulnerable people such as pregnant and nursing mothers, the elderly, babies and young children to avoid uncooked or lightly cooked dishes made with eggs. Once prepared these dishes should be kept refrigerated and used promptly.

Milk should be full fat unless otherwise stated.

Fresh herbs should be used unless otherwise stated. If unavailable use dried herbs as an alternative but halve the quantities stated.

Ovens should be preheated to the specific temperature – if using a fan-assisted oven, follow manufacturer's instructions for adjusting the time and the temperature.

Pepper should be freshly ground black pepper unless otherwise stated.

This book includes dishes made with nuts and nut derivatives. It is advisable for customers with known allergic reactions to nuts and nut derivatives and those who may be potentially vulnerable to these allergies, such as babies and children with a family history of allergies, to avoid dishes made with nuts and nut oils. It is also prudent to check the labels of pre-prepared ingredients for the possible inclusion of nut derivatives.

Vegetarians should look for the 'V' symbol on a cheese to ensure it is made with vegetarian rennet.

Also Available

Recipes for Savoury Bakes

Recipes for Soups

Recipes for Summer